The Good Grammar Guide

Does grammar bother you? Does it inspire first boredom, then fear? Since the virtual removal forty years ago of formal grammar teaching from our schools' standard curriculum, such negative responses have increasingly characterised students and professionals alike. As this lively and accessible book sets out to prove, that is both unfortunate and unnecessary. Not only is grammar an enabling servant rather than a tyrannical set of absolute rules: it can also be **fun**.

The Good Grammar Guide offers extensive coverage of Parts of Speech, Syntax, Inflection and Punctuation, along with a detailed look at common errors and misconceptions. Regular exercises are included, as is a detailed glossary of technical terms, and its finale offers a baleful survey of Politically Correct usage, whose desire to sanitize and control the way we speak is injurious to grammar, language itself and indeed the way we live now.

In keeping with its governing premise –

> Grammar *serves* language: it has done and it always will do. It has never been, nor should ever be, the other way round.

– the aim throughout is to reassure and entertain as well as instruct. Indeed, although this handy volume may not be the most comprehensive guide available, it has a strong claim to be considered the most amusing, and as such it is guaranteed to banish both boredom and fear.

Though entirely discreet, **The Good Grammar Guide** can additionally be read as a companion to the author's **Write in Style**, also published in Routledge's Study Guides series.

Richard Palmer is Head of ⌐ ⌐ author of **Brain Train: Studying for** e to Good **English, 2nd Edition**.

Other titles from Routledge

Brain Train
Studying for success
2nd Edition
Richard Palmer

Effective Speaking
Communicating in speech
Christopher Turk

Effective Writing
Improving scientific, technical and
business communications
2nd Edition
Christopher Turk and John Kirkman

Good Style
Writing for science and
technology
John Kirkman

How to Get an MBA
Morgen Witzel

Scientists Must Write
A guide to better writing for
scientists, engineers and students
2nd Edition
Robert Barrass

Students Must Write
A guide to better writing in
coursework and examinations
2nd Edition
Robert Barrass

Study!
A guide to effective study,
revision and examination
techniques
2nd Edition
Robert Barrass

Writing at Work
A guide to better writing in
administration, business and
management
Robert Barrass

For more information about these and other titles published by Routledge
please contact:

Routledge, 11 New Fetter Lane, London EC4P 4EE.
Tel: 020 7583 9855; Fax: 020 7842 2303; or visit our web site at
www.Routledge.com

The Good Grammar Guide

Richard Palmer

Routledge
Taylor & Francis Group

LONDON AND NEW YORK

First published 2003
by Routledge
11 New Fetter Lane, London EC4P 4EE

Simultaneously published in the USA and Canada
by Routledge
29 West 35th Street, New York, NY 10001

Reprinted 2004

Routledge is an imprint of the Taylor & Francis Group

© 2003 Richard Palmer

Typeset in Goudy by
Keystroke, Jacaranda Lodge, Wolverhampton
Printed and bound in Great Britain by
TJ International Ltd, Padstow, Cornwall

British Library Cataloguing in Publication Data
A catalogue record for this book is available
from the British Library

Library of Congress Cataloging in Publication Data
A catalog record for this book has been requested

ISBN 0–415–31226–4

To Roger and Helen Allen

Contents

List of exercises

Preface

Why care for grammar so long as we are good?

Artemus Ward

Whoever you are, it is most unlikely that you will go through this or any other day without hearing someone – it may even be you – mention the word **stress**. The notion that all of us are under more or less constant pressure has come to dominate our culture; indeed, to hear some people talk you'd think we *invented*

**. . . the heartache and the thousand natural shocks
That flesh is heir to.**

Not so, of course. Those words are spoken by perhaps the most stressed-out character in all literature – Shakespeare's Hamlet – and they are a timeless reminder that 'the stresses and strains of modern living' have applied to every generation since *Homo sapiens* evolved.

Nevertheless, a case could still be made for **stress** as the defining word of our time. One consequence – or maybe index – of that is the profusion of surveys tabulating the most common causes of stress and/or their degree of severity. If my sampling of such items has been reliable, the two greatest would appear to be moving house and speaking in public. The latter topped a fairly recent poll addressing people's worst fears, weighing in at an impressive 40 per cent; **dying** could do no better than third place, which I find, in the legendary words of David Coleman, 'really quite remarkable'.

It would be idle to suggest that grammar competes with domestic transformation, speechifying or death as a cause of stress or fear, but try this simple game anyway. Take a piece of paper and at the top of it write the word

grammar.

Then beneath it write down the first few things that come into your head as you consider that word. (If you prefer, you can log them mentally instead.)

All done? Now, if you've bought this book, or even if you've picked it up for a cursory browse, its subject is presumably not without interest or importance to you, so it's unlikely that anything on your list suggests either outright dread or boredom – not uncommon reactions from others! Even so, I'd be surprised if at least some of your associations are not on the negative side. Grammar may not induce the highest stress-levels, but it *bothers* people. I want to spend a few moments investigating why that should be so, and I begin with the schooldays of one of England's favourite sons, Sir Winston Churchill (1874–1965).

'Winston Churchill Learns Latin' forms Chapter 11 of the finest book on teaching I have yet read, Jonathan Smith's *The Learning Game*.[1] Reproducing a passage from Churchill's *My Early Life*, it offers a definitive portrait of education at its worst; in the circumstances it would be inappropriate to speak of highlights, but the much-reduced extract which follows should be enough to curdle the blood. You need to know that Churchill has been given half an hour to learn the first declension –

Mensa	a table	*nominative*[2]
Mensa	O table	*vocative*
Mensam	a table	*accusative*
Mensae	of a table	*genitive*
Mensae	to or for a table	*dative*
Mensa	by, with or from a table	*ablative*

– and that the hapless novice, finding it all an 'absolute rigmarole', falls back on his ability to learn things by heart. The master then returns:

> 'Have you learnt it?' he asked.
> 'I think I can *say* it, sir,' I replied; and I gabbled it off.
> He seemed so satisfied with this that I was emboldened to ask a question.

1 Published by Little, Brown in 2000 and later in paperback (2002). In 2001 it featured in Radio 4's series *Book of the Week*.
2 This column lists the **case** of each word. Do not be concerned if you don't understand that term or the six words themselves: they are explored in Chapter One and also in Chapter Three.

'What does it mean, sir?'

'Mensa means a table,' he answered.

'Then why does mensa also mean O table,' I enquired, 'and what does O table mean?'

'Mensa, O table, is the vocative case,' he replied . . . 'You would use it in speaking to a table.'

'But I never do,' I blurted out in honest amazement.

'If you are impertinent, you will be punished, and punished, let me tell you, very severely . . .'

My immediate reaction to that – I trust it's yours too – is that the master emerges as barking mad, and that even by the educational standards of the time (the episode must have taken place in the 1880s) it is a scandal that he was allowed anywhere near a classroom. But the story is disturbing in a much broader fashion, one which far outweighs the 'local' insanity that supposes the correct way of addressing a table to constitute an important life skill. It enshrines a philosophy that regards grammar as entirely a set of rules, as a formulaic system whose authority is supreme, and which has *an absolute value* regardless of context or use. And that flies ruinously in the face of a fundamental principle which I shall reiterate more than once:

Grammar *serves* language: it always has done and it always will do. It has never been, nor should ever be, the other way round.

The chronic failure to recognise that and act on it in our classrooms eventually led to a development in the 1960s[3] whose (dire) consequences are with us still. Purely by virtue of when I was born, I escaped those, and while autobiographical reminiscence may seem out of place in a technical manual, a brief account of how that came about and how things then changed should throw some light on why this *Guide* is in your hand.

By the time I entered Dulwich College in 1958 at the age of eleven, I had already been taught a good deal of rudimentary grammar at primary school, and that aspect of English continued to be central to how I was taught as a secondary pupil. It grew in sophistication, naturally, and it was bolstered by a similar focus in my instruction in French, Latin and (later) German. In the main my teachers were very good – light years away from the tyrannical cretin whom Churchill encountered – and by

3 Coincidentally, just about the time when Churchill died at the grand old age of 91.

the time I took 'O' Level English Language I was adept at parsing, declension and conjugation, précis, clause analysis and all the rest of it.

I have two observations to make about that part of my education. The first is that I came to be deeply grateful that I had been helped to such knowledge, and not just because I went on to be an English teacher myself. And the second is that at the time

I just *hated* it.

My memories are almost solely those of tiresome rote-learning, labrynthine notes dictated with tablets-of-stone religiosity, and a seemingly endless array of fustian exercises designed to ensure you could distinguish **subordinate** from **subjunctive** and know your parse from your elbow.[4] Grammar was about as far removed from the concept of enjoyment as it was possible to conceive: indeed, the two things seemed to be implacable enemies.[5]

And that is surely why, shortly after I'd moved on from 'O' Level to the real joys of English, grammar teaching in schools very rapidly became a thing of the past. The mid-1960s in England was a time of great upheaval and flux – in sexual mores, pop music, fashion, politics, you name it – and with hindsight it figures that equally seismic changes should overtake the world of education. The key players in this 'revolution' were not educational philosophers or administrators, think-tank radicals or

---

4 Should any crusty purist be reading this, I am aware that my usage here is illegitimate: **parse** is not a noun but a transitive verb. Other readers might wish to know that **to parse** is 'to resolve a sentence into its component parts and describe them grammatically.'

5 There was one memorable exception to this – third form Latin. Our teacher frightened the life out of us for a few weeks but then became an almost boundless source of amusement, though he would have been mortified had he known it. His teaching style hinged on a raft of phrases constantly evident – 'commonest word in the language'; 'Poo-urr (i.e. Poor) ! Not good enough! Do it again a couple of times!'; 'your translation was garbled and inaccurate' – all delivered in a fortissimo Bristolian burr which never failed to give us the giggles. The highlight, however, was the teaching of '*ut*' plus the subjunctive to indicate 'a clause of purpose' and its cousin '*ne*' plus the subjunctive to indicate a clause of negative purpose, as in the English **lest**.' His invariable illustration went, phonetically rendered: 'I went *tuh* London *tah* see the Queen.' To this day I cannot hear the words '*ut*', '*ne*' or 'to see the Queen' without breaking into a grin or open laughter. And that is extremely important. The hilarity such moments inspired was a crucial aid to our learning: I will go to my grave knowing about *ut* and the subjunctive as well as I know my own phone number, because he made Latin grammar *fun*. True, that that was never his intention; however, it is mine in this book, and fundamentally so.

even the students themselves.[6] They were the *teachers*, especially (though not solely) teachers of English. Terminally fed up with middle-school syllabuses that were joyless to teach and largely sterile in effect, they looked to transform lessons into something that was fun, encouraging and developing pupils' creativity, imagination and awareness of the world around them. Out went grammar and a dependence on the canon of 'improving' literature; in came a greatly increased premium on creative writing, the use of radio and television material, drama, the seeds of what would become known as multimedia activity and a governing emphasis on oral communication and the enabling pleasures of speech.

In all respects but one I have nothing but admiration for those initiatives. Moreover, I am as much in their debt as I am to those teachers who earlier ensured my mechanical soundness. By the time I entered the profession in the early 1970s, such practice and its attendant values were firmly established, and I realised with delight that there was virtually *nothing* that could not serve as a productive and enjoyable source for an English lesson. That has continued to be the case throughout my career, and my gratitude is immense.

My single reservation is nonetheless an enormous one. The consequent abandonment of grammar as a regular or even visible constituent of English teaching has been cumulatively disastrous. A whole generation grew up virtually ignorant of how language actually works, and the situation is no better for its successor. Why else would a Literacy Hour now be considered essential in all primary schools? Why else would a major commercial organisation think it necessary to hire someone like me to teach established and able professionals the rudiments of grammar and essential mechanical skills? Why else, indeed, is this book considered marketable?

I detest the cliché 'throwing the baby out with the bathwater',[7] but I fear it is all too apposite in this instance. The baby in this instance was grammar itself, or the need to know it; the bathwater was the *way* it had traditionally been taught. To confuse substance and style may have been understandable at the time, but it was no less damaging for that. Moreover, that either/or approach, far from abating over the years, has become ever more entrenched (such initiatives as the Literacy Hour

---

6   That came later, especially in Paris in the spring of 1968.
7   Partly because I'm not clear as to what it means – or rather because I cannot imagine anybody ever expelling a loved infant in the process of emptying its bath any more than I can envisage an adult human being 'crying over spilt milk'.

notwithstanding). It is still commonplace to hear **grammar** and **creativity** proposed as opposites, whereas of course they are vital complements to each other – an irrefutable case of both/and. Nobody ever wants to read meticulously accurate prose that is fully as exciting as looking up the word 'anorak' in a dictionary; neither, however, does anyone want to peruse a piece that may abound in creative energy but whose bypassing of punctuation, syntax and other such mechanical properties quickly renders its meaning impossible to decipher. What we all want – don't we? – is prose with plenty to say and a vigorous way of saying it that is immediately and enjoyably clear. That synthesis is what grammar enables, as S. H. Burton's admirable definition confirms:

> **Grammar is not a collection of hard-and-fast rules. It is more flexible (and, therefore, more useful) than that. Grammar gives an account of the way in which a language is used by those who use it well.**[8]

Yet the fact remains that (to return to my beginning) grammar *bothers* people. It makes them nervous, diffident, vulnerable, provoking intimations of ignorance, even illiteracy. Unsurprisingly, therefore, it can inspire the same mixture of fear and dismissive contempt that characterise making a will, going to the dentist or completing one's tax return. However, that last analogy brings to mind a television advertising campaign that the Inland Revenue mounted recently, featuring the slogan

'It's never as bad as you think.'

I hope I can persuade you that the same is true of grammar, and that knowing more about how your language works will benefit you both as a writer and a reader, especially the latter: as an ex-pupil of mine, now a fine teacher, puts it –

> **I certainly agree with all the research that having a knowledge of the metalanguage[9] may not make you a better *writer*, but I am absolutely convinced that it does make you a more perceptive and critical *reader* – both of non-fiction and literary texts.**[10]

8 In *Mastering English Language* (London: Macmillan, 1982) p. 128.
9 **Metalanguage:** The language used when talking or writing about language itself.
10 Robert Kapadia in a letter to the author, August 6, 2002.

I do not claim to offer an exhaustive guide to every conceivable grammatical point. What follows does nevertheless cover most things that students and writers will need to know in the course of their normal work. If you require a comprehensive treatment, there is still nothing finer than Fowler's *Modern English Usage*, and I list other recommended works in Appendix III: Further Reading.

Right, let's get under way. And let's look to have some *fun* as we go.

Acknowledgements

As will shortly become evident, this book is in part a companion volume to the (2002) revised edition of my *Write In Style*. I would like to re-thank all the individuals and institutions cited in that publication's acknowledgements anyway, because their influence, contribution and friendship attend this volume too. Since, however, this is now a discrete work, I want to pay affectionate and grateful tribute to those who had a direct impact on the chapters that follow.

I am very grateful to my good friends and/or colleagues Roger Allen, Colin Brezicki, John Fleming, Andrew Grimshaw, Robert Kapadia, Brendan Law, Wendy Pollard, Jane Richardson and Mike and Louise Tucker for helpfully critical and enabling suggestions, interest and support, and to Jonathan Smith, whose inspirational *The Learning Game* taught me a great deal very fast. And I am especially indebted to Louise Berridge, a brilliant ex-student of mine who crucially apprised me of the Anglo-Saxon genitive's relevance to the use of the apostrophe.

I want also to thank Jackie Max and Tim Raynor of NatWest Bank's IT Learning and Development operation. They engaged me to teach grammar and all its related issues to successive cadres of able professionals who felt they had missed out on grammar schooling in their earlier years. No less warm is my gratitude to Eddie and Janet Cook, under whose editorishop of *Teeline* magazine I wrote a monthly column on English Usage from 1986–94.

I owe another and considerable debt to my daughter Jo, whose observations about the Literacy Hour have proved invaluable in my own efforts in that area. She is a primary-school teacher whose every hour features things I could never imagine coping with, let alone triumphing in, as she does, and that has proved as instructive as humbling.

Authors thank their editors as a matter of course and courtesy, so I want to say that this tribute to Anna Clarkson and Louise Mellor is on a quite different level. They are, quite simply, the best team I have ever worked with and for, and in so far as this book succeeds, it is as much down to their efforts and quality as my own.

The last acknowledgement is to my wife Ann. Every thing about this book and all else I've attempted as an author would not have been possible without her tolerance, her support and her love, but above all without her.

A brief note on the text

This book started life as a hundred-page 'Grammar Primer' that formed Part Five of my 1993 *Write In Style: A Guide To Good English*. When a revised edition of that work was proposed in 2000, a strong case emerged for dropping that material and publishing it in discrete form instead.

Two considerations governed that initiative, the first frankly commercial. Although there were a few deletions from the original edition, revising the manuscript of *Write In Style* turned out to be chiefly an exercise in expansion, and it became clear that unless something in the order of those hundred pages could be excised, Routledge would be unable to retail it at a competitive price. The second hinged on readers' needs rather than raw sales – a more edifying concern even though the two are obviously connected! I had come to realise that some of those who might consult *Write in Style* for its chapters on (say) the art of paragraphing or the writing of reports were by no means certain to need fundamental or even sophisticated advice on grammar. Conversely, not all of those who were primarily interested in the latter would find some of the earlier material entirely pertinent. Two separate volumes seemed more desirable as well as expedient.

And so *The Good Grammar Guide* was born. It is notably larger than its precursor: Chapters One and Seven are completely new, as is Appendix I; additions have been made to Chapters Four and Five; the number of exercises has also increased. Finally, although this *Guide* is now a stand-alone publication, I hope its pages may encourage readers to investigate the Revised *Write In Style*, for the books are still designed to complement each other.

Chapter 1

Introduction
Finding your feet

I have just spent some time considering the ways in which grammar can be an intimidating matter for those many people who feel that they are not entirely competent in it. So although it would be perfectly feasible to examine grammatical terms and their functions straightaway, I am not going to do that. Many such terms are difficult and unhelpful even to those who know what they signify, and I suspect that anyone who has picked up this book looking for enlightenment would not find such an immediately technical approach all that helpful. In keeping with the governing principle outlined in my Preface –

> **Language – including and especially everyday usage – does not serve grammar: it is the other way round**

– I propose instead to give you some immediate hands-on experience of how grammar works in practice.

1.1 GETTING STARTED

Below follows a brief narrative of my own devising. It contains thirty real or alleged errors of varying kinds, including wrong or suspect use of words; mistakes in word order; errors in agreement and number; confusion and ambiguity; faulty use of cases. If some of those terms make little or no sense to you, please do not worry and do not stop reading! All the points in question are numbered as the piece unfolds, and full explanations are offered afterwards. Individual readers have their own needs and ways of going about things, so if you at once want to check the 'mistake' with the explanation, fine; you might, however, prefer to think about what is wrong in each instance and how it might be put right before consulting my observations.

Some of the errors are easy or obvious; some others are more subtle, even tricky. And as telegraphed, some of them are not errors at all but rooted in mere prejudice. For example, the sentence you've just read breaks a 'rule' that has never existed:

One should never begin a sentence with a conjunction.

This widespread belief is entirely mistaken and a sadly eloquent example of how misguided grammar teaching can harm style and communication rather than enable it. An analogous phoney rule is that

It is always wrong to end a sentence with a preposition.

Instances of both alleged errors appear in the piece. A justification of my impatience with their wrong-headedness appears in the explanatory gloss, as does advice about where full chapter and verse on the matters at issue can be found in subsequent sections of the book. Finally, you should know that on this occasion there are no intentional mistakes in either spelling or punctuation.

Exercise I

Who do I get in touch with? (1) Everyone's disinterested. (2) Here we are, in the middle of the biggest and longest rain-storm the village has ever known, threatening to decimate (3) our crops, our houses, our drains, our everything, and none of the inhabitants are (4) doing anything about it. The English pride themselves on their stoicism when it comes to the weather, but it seems like (5) this lot have mortgaged their (6) brains, trotting out idiocies such as 'It'll blow over soon' or 'I'm bored of (7) your panic talk.' I'm tempted to just wash (8) my hands of the whole thing – an appropriate image under the circumstances (9).

Between you and I (10), a major crisis is brewing. I never have and I never will see (11) such rain: already the roads are permanently awash, and it wouldn't surprise me to see someone floating down the High Street in an armchair. But (12) I can't get anyone to take me seriously. 'What are you talking about?' (13) the Fire & Rescue Officer said. 'It's no different than (14) last

continued

year's June storms, and after that (15) we had weeks of unbroken sunshine.' He seemed oblivious to (16) the enormity (17) of water cascading passed (18) his window as he spoke those words; he also appeared insensible of (19) the faint but definite splash that his boots made when he walked across the floor. Mind you, the Police had even fewer intelligence. (20) 'Speaking professionally, I prefer the rain than (21) the sun,' the Duty Constable told me. 'When it's wet the kids stay indoors and commit less nuisances (22). We haven't had a crime reported in five days: that's quite unique (23).'

I suppose such positive thinking has its admirable side, but such an attitude mitigates against (24) the fact that in another five days there may not be a village left to commit any crime in (25). The only person talking sense is the Village Postmistress. As a woman, I don't find her very attractive (26) but I warm to her masterful (27) analysis of the situation: 'If we don't get a State of Emergency declared soon,' she insists, 'the rain will not only threaten our livelihoods but also our very lives. (28) Why won't someone act rather than just laying down?' (29) At least we both know how Noah must of (30) felt.

Answers and explanations

Note: a term appearing in **bold italics** denotes one that is fully explained elswhere in this book. If necessary, consult the Index and/or the Glossary that forms Appendix I.

1 It is often argued that to end a sentence with a **preposition** – in this case **with** – is always bad practice. As noted above, I have no time for that idea. It is true, yes, that you should not make a regular habit of it; on the other hand, avoiding it *on principle* can create bloated and unpleasing phrasing. The alternative here would be 'With whom do I get in touch?', which strikes me as both pompous and ugly, as do such analogous structures as 'To what is the world coming?' or 'I don't know to where he is going.'

2 A very common error even amongst professional writers. **Disinterested** does not mean 'bored': it means 'neutral' or 'impartial'. The word required here is **uninterested**.

3 Derived from the Latin for 'ten', **decimate** means 'to kill one in every

ten'. It should not be used as a (bogus) synonym for 'destroy' or 'devastate'.

4 **None** is a singular structure and should therefore be followed by a singular verb ('is'), not a plural one ('are'). See **Number** in Chapters 1 and 3.

5 Strictly speaking, **like** should not be used as a conjunction, as it has been here: the more correct structure would be 'it seems **as if** . . .'. However, this is one of those 'rules' that usage seems to have rendered redundant: so many writers use 'like' in this way that it has become accepted. Personally I regret that, for I find such use of 'like' falls unpleasantly on the ear, but no doubt that's just the middle-aged pedant in me.

6 **This lot** is a *collective noun* and as such is singular; therefore the *possessive adjective* ought to be 'its', not 'their'.

7 A recent illiteracy that is as ugly as unnecessary. The term is **bored with**, not **of**.

8 **To just wash** is a *split infinitive*. Grammatical purists consider it bad practice to insert anything between the 'to' and the verb in question, and in the main they are right, as the resultant structure harms the rhythm and elegance of what's being said. But it would be unwise to be obsessive about it: the instance in question does no damage to clarity or *euphony*,[1] and sometimes it is *essential* to split an infinitive to communicate the desired meaning. 'I want you to really work' differs significantly from 'I really want you to work' or even 'I want you really to work', which admits of two meanings.

9 **In the circumstances**, not **under**. 'Circumstances' refers to things that surround: you can't get 'under' surroundings.

10 **Between you and *me***, of course. **Between** is a *preposition*, and all prepositions in English take the *accusative case*. (See the section on *Cases* later in this chapter.) Though an elementary mistake, it is surprising how often one encounters it, and one of the reasons is sheer snobbery. Somehow the idea has grown up that it is socially superior to use **I** rather than the 'proletarian' **me**. If words are an army, then **I** is officer class while **me** belongs to the ranks. Such pretension is all the more disagreeable for being entirely wrong!

---

1 'Euphony' comes from two Greek words meaning 'good' and 'sound', and thus means 'the quality of sounding pleasant'; analogously, the adjective **euphonious** indicates 'attractive to the ear'. It is a fundamental consideration, every bit as important as formalistic rules and sometimes more so.

11 The first verb is incomplete: it needs the participle **seen** after it, since the second, linked verb ends in **see**, which cannot complete the **never have** structure. This is a subtle matter known as *ellipsis*: it is easily done in the heat of composition, but it can cause confusion or obscurity and thus needs careful monitoring.

12 Not an error. Provided one uses the practice sparingly, it is perfectly in order to begin sentences with conjunctions: for one thing, the resultant capital emphasises the word in a way not possible in normal circumstances, and sometimes one desires such a stress. That principle is even more important with **and**, which is so common a word as to be almost invisible in the normal run of things: using it to start a sentence is an admirable way to ensure that its added significance in this particular instance is established at once. Used with discretion it can be a very valuable tool.[2]

13 Another example of justifiably ending a sentence with a preposition. The structure here is clearly preferable to the clumsy alternative, 'About what are you talking?'

14 **Different *from***. The oft-encountered 'different to' is bad enough, but 'different than' – which appears to have been imported from the USA – is just ghastly. In the main I am a great admirer of American English, which can often be superior to its UK counterpart in both precision and vitality, but 'different than' is as absurd as it is ugly. The verb from which **different** derives is **differ**: no one would say 'I differ *to* you in this', let alone 'I differ *than* you in this', so why these adjectival illiteracies have emerged is a mystery. Illiteracies they remain, however; avoid them!

15 Terribly picky, I admit, but since the previous noun is a plural (**storms**) the pronoun ought to be **those**, not **that**. See *Number*.

16 **Oblivious *of***, not **to**.

17 **Enormity** is *not* an alternative for 'enormousness' or any noun denoting great size. It means 'monstrous wickedness' or 'unspeakable crime', a meaning worth preserving. Here, use 'colossal volume' or better still, 'magnitude'.

---

2 The *Second Book of Samuel* is a spectacular examplar of just how effective this device can be. Chapter 11 (in the 1611 Authorised Version) tells the story of David's passion for Bathsheba and his eventually successful attempt to deal with the problem of her husband, Uriah the Hittite. Of its twenty-seven verses, only three do not begin with a conjunction, and of the remaining twenty-four, twenty-two begin with **And**. That may seem excessive, and it is probably not a model to follow in full! But the tale moves forward with riveting authority, and those relentless conjunctions are partly the reason for such power.

18 **Past**, not **passed**. The latter is used only when the past tense of **pass** is required; all other uses require 'past'. And yes, that is of necessity a rather tortuous, headache-inducing explanation – which is perhaps why the error is made as often as it is!

19 **Insensible *to*, not *of*.**

20 **Less**, not **fewer**. **Less** is used with singular nouns, **fewer** with plural ones – always. 'Fewer brains' would be all right; see also number 22 below.

21 **Prefer the rain *to* the sun**, not **than**. Not quite as bad as 'different than' above, perhaps, but still illiterate.

22 **Fewer**, not **less** – the reverse companion to number 20. Here we have a plural noun, **nuisances**, so **fewer** is required. 'Less crime' would be all right.

23 Something is either **unique** or it isn't: the word means 'one of a kind' and cannot therefore be qualified. So 'quite unique' is an absurdity, even if 'very unique' is even sillier.

24 The doubly illiterate **mitigates against** is disturbingly prevalent these days, not least because so many top-class professionals imagine it makes any kind of sense. It does not: **mitigate** means 'to appease, to lessen, to soften' – as in the phrase 'mitigating circumstances' – and none of those verbs can possibly be accompanied by **against**. Somewhere along the line, it would seem, **mitigate** has been confused with **militate**, which invariably is used with **against** and means 'to have force, to be telling'.

25 A further instance of ending a sentence with a preposition. On this occasion the alternative . . . 'a village left in which to commit any crime' is entirely *euphonious* and therefore just as good; however, placing the in at the very end gives it additional emphasis, which is what the thrust of the remark seems to require. I would therefore keep it as it is.

26 Assuming the speaker to be male, **As a woman** sets up a comic confusion; even if the speaker were female, it would still be clumsy and, for want of a better word, wrong. The sense intended here is 'I don't find her very attractive as a woman' and that is the structure required: as it stands, it is an example of the *displaced nominative* or *hanging descriptor*, the effects of which are almost always injurious to both meaning and dignity. Such slips are easily made, however, and one needs to be on the watch for them.

27 Another very common error. There are two meanings of the noun 'master' – 1 Boss; 2. Expert – and each meaning has its attendant adjective. **Masterful** means 'authoritative' in the sense of 'bossy',

'domineering' or, less unpleasantly, 'completely in control'; **masterly** means 'authoritative' in the sense of 'expert', 'highly accomplished', 'excellent'. In this context, **masterly** is clearly the right, intended meaning.

28 Again rather picky, but the two *correlatives* **not only** and **but also** should introduce the same part of speech, and that is not the case here: **not only** prefaces the verb 'threaten' while **but also** prefaces the noun 'lives'. Ideally it should be rewritten as 'the rain will threaten not only our livelihoods but also our very lives'.

29 *Lying* down, not **laying**. This is an easy trap to fall into, for a number of reasons.

   Lay also happens to be the past tense of **lie**; in addition, American usage increasingly ignores the original distinction between **lie** (*intransitive*: = 'to be prone') and **lay** (*transitive*: = 'to place, deposit, arrange') and many non-Americans seem to be following suit. Indeed, in their fine *Introducing English Grammar*, Börjars and Burridge argue that 'It is time to switch off the life-support system for the **lay-lie** distinction . . . the price of maintaining it is just too high.'³ Although I suspect this view will eventually prevail, it is not one I share, and the matter is further explored in Chapter Three below, pp. 67–8.

30 One of the most common (in both senses) illiteracies of all. It should of course be **must have**; if the abbreviated form is desired, then write *must've*.

1.2 GETTING SOME BEARINGS

The remainder of this chapter is devoted to a preliminary look at some fundamental grammatical terms. Some readers may feel they do not require such a guide, in which case they should move on to the next chapter; others, even if they are familiar with some of the material covered, may find it an additionally helpful lead-in. In any event, all the matters addressed are explored more extensively later on, and the sequence adopted here is purely alphabetical.

1 Apostrophe

This word has two meanings, derived from different Greek roots. The first – unlikely to be needed or indeed encountered very often – denotes 'a declamatory or exclamatory address, directed at someone present, absent or even dead'; from this we get the verb *to apostrophise*. It is of course the second meaning that will chiefly concern nearly all of you, the punctuation device (') that signals 'the omission of one or more letters in a word'.

The apostrophe is almost certainly the most abused, least understood device in the entire spectrum of English punctuation and grammar. It is regularly used when it shouldn't be and equally often omitted when its use is mandatory. I offer chapter and verse on this in Chapters Five and Seven; for now let me advertise arguably the most important point of all:

> **It is often maintained that there are two 'kinds' of apostrophe – one denoting omission, the other possession.**

False. The so-called 'possessive apostrophe' hinges on omission just as much as all the others. When we write

> **the boy's bicycle   the woman's handbag   the swallows' nests**

in each case the **'s** is the now-truncated form of the original Anglo Saxon genitive ending **-es**, and

> **It is that surviving genitive case that signals possession, not the apostrophe itself.**

Pedantic? Possibly; yet in my experience the reason why so many children and nearly as many adults get into such a mess over apostrophes is that they've no real idea what the symbol means and/or why they're using it. Once it is firmly grasped that *all* apostrophes denote an omitted letter and that you should never use one unless a letter *is* being omitted, there's a good chance that accurate usage will ensue.

2 Case

Compared to several European languages, English is not highly inflected;[4] as a result, *visible* instances of **case** are much less frequent in English than

---

4 An inflection means a change in the form of a word according to the job it is doing.

in (say) Latin or German, where the endings of words change according to the case being used. Such changes do regularly occur in English pronouns, but the vast majority of our nouns and adjectives remain the same regardless of the case in question. However, every writer ought to be familiar with the **five cases** that operate in English, for two reasons. First, the case-structure is still there even if it is not visible; second, the more you know about what is going on in a sentence, the more likely you are both to understand it to the full and write with comparable assurance when it comes to your turn. The five cases are:

The nominative case   The case of a noun or pronoun when it functions as the **subject** of a verb:
She **arrives on Good Friday.**
They **destroyed the evidence.**

The vocative case   The case that is used when addressing a person or thing:
Now, *sir*, what is your problem?
***Mum*, where are my trainers?**

We looked earlier[5] at Winston Churchill's account of the way he was instructed in the vocative case when at Harrow, and if you found that story as appalling as I intended, you could be forgiven for dismissing the whole vocative issue as a waste of time, not to say alarmingly imbecilic. That would be a mistake. It is of course perfectly true that only those in serious need of medical treatment go around saying 'O table!' or for that matter 'O trees!' or 'O flowers!'; nor indeed is the structure 'O . . .' used anywhere outside dramatic literature and opera. But vocatives are more common in English than many seem to be aware, and they require meticulous punctuation. I've lost count of the number of times I've read such remarks as 'This is a fine essay Tim' or 'You've let yourself down badly George', where the vocatives 'Tim' and 'George' *must* be separated by a comma from the rest of the structure, since they bear no grammatical relation to it.[6] At best such flaws are lazy, at worst ignorant, and they are

---

5   See *Preface* above, pp. xii–xiii.
6   That is to say, the sentences would have exactly the same meaning if the vocatives were removed. Their *tone* would be more impersonal, and it could be argued that the deletion of 'Tim' and 'George' sacrifices certain *information*; nevertheless, the governing import of the remarks is entirely unchanged. In that respect, vocatives are like **interjections**, a Part of Speech defined in the next chapter; they require similarly exact punctuation.

perpetrated daily by even professional writers and teachers. They may not be outlandish errors, but like any mistake they still matter.

The accusative case   The case of a noun or pronoun when it denotes the **direct object** of a verb
I saw *her* this evening.
or when it is governed by a preposition
I was invited by *them*.

As observed in the thirty-point exercise earlier in this chapter, *all* English prepositions take the accusative case.

The genitive case   The case of a noun or pronoun when it denotes that something *belongs* to a person or thing
He had been eating too many of Mr *Kipling's* cakes.
She trod on *the cat's* tail.

The genitive case is usually the easiest to identify, because of the **'s** structure. A reminder, however: the apostrophe here still denotes omission – in this case that of the **e** in the Anglo-Saxon genitive suffix **es**.

The dative case	The case of a noun or pronoun when it denotes the **indirect object**[7] of a verb: **She gave *him* a present on her birthday** **He sent *the President* a letter-bomb.**

3 Clause

A group of words that has a subject and predicate[8] –

The plane will take off when the fog clears.

where 'the plane will take off' and 'when the fog clears' are clauses.

This is not an easy topic, and we shall return to it. For now, you need to be aware that clauses are either **main** or **subordinate**. The former is a structure that can stand on its own, as in the first clause in the above example:

The plane will take off.

A subordinate clause may be just as interesting or important in terms of the information it gives, but it is dependent on the main clause for its meaning: it cannot stand on its own. Thus the second clause above

When the fog clears . . .

is subordinate in that it is not complete, needing further information to make it so.

A sentence comprising a main clause and one or more subordinate clauses is known as a **complex sentence**.[9]

---

7   There is a discrete section on the **indirect object** in Chapter Seven (7.4).
8   Don't worry about this term: though forbidding, in effect it simply means 'everything in the sentence or clause apart from the subject'. By definition, 'predicate' includes a **finite verb**; if that term also bothers you, it is addressed shortly in item 10 of this list.
9   See Chapter Four, pp. 81–5.

4 Complement

This term means 'that which completes', and it occurs only with verbs of *being*, *becoming* or *appearing*. Those verbs do not – cannot – take an object, but in many cases they also do not make complete sense on their own. I suppose you could argue that

I am.

does make complete sense: it announces that I exist. But the same could not be said of

She becomes.   They appear.   We seem.

– all of which require an addition to be meaningful.

To be candid, **complement** is one of several grammatical terms that I find myself getting annoyed about from time to time: others include **adjective**, the just-mentioned **predicate** and the imminent **correlatives**. They can seem needlessly difficult, as if their chief purpose is to confuse or obscure. Fortunately, there's nothing difficult about **complement** in practice. The complement simply fulfils the function performed by the direct object in sentences with transitive verbs. The difference is that you could 'reverse' the two components of a sentence containing a complement without any change in meaning –

1a He is an accountant.   1b An accountant is he.

1b is much clumsier than 1a, of course, and it is not an alternative anyone would recommend for other than comic purposes. But though elegance is sacrificed, meaning is unaltered – whereas if you 'reversed' a sentence featuring a **direct object**, meaning would be transformed:

2a The crowd clapped the players.
2b The players clapped the crowd.
3a The hunter shot the elephant.
3b The elephant shot the hunter.

2b's *meaning* is perfectly feasible while 3b's is ridiculous, but they both illustrate the fact that you cannot turn round transitive sentences in such a fashion. Even if what you end up with isn't nonsense, it is still decisively different from what you want to say. So if in any doubt about whether you're dealing with a **complement** or not, try that 'reversal principle': it should clarify things very quickly.

5 Correlatives

Correlatives are words or phrases that are used together, always in pairs, and so related that one component implies the other:

> either . . . or   neither . . . nor   both . . . and   not only . . . but also

6 Demonstrative adjective

A rather bossy-looking term, but it becomes pleasantly straightforward if you bear in mind the verb *demonstrate*. These adjectives *point* to a noun, their application is limited to the person or thing identified –

> *this* village   *that* field   *those* cattle

7 Demonstrative pronoun

The same principles as for 6. These pronouns highlight a particular object or concept:

> *This* is how I feel   *That* is my Jaguar

8 Distributives

Adjectives and pronouns that refer to each individual of a class:

> each   every   other

9 Ellipsis

The definition of this term in the *Shorter Oxford English Dictionary* is:

> **The omission of one or more words in a sentence, which would be needed to express the sense completely**

and that is the function you will come across or use most often.

Such omission is sometimes 'unsignalled': it is assumed that the reader can silently supply the missing words:

James is learning Spanish, and Simon French

There the words *is learning* are understood to appear after Simon; such an assumption also attends the use of imperative verbs –

come here   stop that   kiss me

– where the placing of the pronoun **You before the verbs** *come*, *stop* and *kiss* is understood.

On other occasions, ellipsis *is* signalled, by three dots: **. . .** If I were to apply ellipsis to the first sentence in this subsection, it might appear as

The definition of this term in the *Shorter Oxford English Dictionary* . . . is the function you will . . . use most often.

The practice allows you to retain the governing sense of a remark while editing it for your own purposes. A small but very neat device, it is invaluable when quoting, especially if you're writing to a word-limit.

But ellipsis has two other applications that the *SOED* does not list – one weak, one strong. The former can be used to signify not just an edited remark but one that is never *finished*. Perhaps the commonest example occurs in dialogue, when one speaker interrupts another:

'What I want . . .'
'I don't care what you want.'

In such a case you could use a dash **(–)** instead, but the latter is so valuable as the equivalent of a strong comma that its integrity in that respect should be preserved. Using this **weak ellipsis** enables you to do so, and it is an elegant method in its own right.

In striking contrast, **the strong ellipsis** is a very weighty pause – a kind of 'big brother' to the paragraph. It is most often used in novels to denote a significant lapse in time; in non-fiction writing it can be a deftly economical way of signalling the need for further thought and action or that the way forward is shrouded in uncertainty:

It would be good to see him heeding this advice . . .
As to what we do next . . .

To be used sparingly anyway, **the strong ellipsis** is unlikely to strike writers engaged on academic or professional tasks as an appropriate device very often, if at all. But it is always worthwhile to know what a punctuation signal denotes, and I would hope that you'll now be comfortable with ellipsis in all its four applications, even if your need is to decode it as a reader rather than use it yourself.

10 Finite verb

This most fundamental of terms troubles an enormous number of students, even very bright ones. I'm not sure why: perhaps it's the word 'finite' that is resistant to understanding – in which case adding the prefix **de** to it to make **definite** may help. For a **finite verb** renders an action or state of being *definite* in two crucial ways: it identifies who or what is in charge of the action (i.e. the **subject**), and it fixes the action in a precise time zone or **tense** – past, present or future. Thus

> *The dog bites* **the milkman.**
> *The bomb destroyed* **the bus-station.**
> *She will marry* **him on Saturday.**

are all finite verbs, having a subject – *the dog, the bomb, she* – and a verb placed in a specific tense – *bites* (present), *destroyed* (past), *will marry* (future).[10]

11 Gender

Gender is the classifying of nouns and pronouns according to the sex of the objects they denote. Unlike Latin, French and German, where every noun is given a gender, the issue does not arise in English all that often; unlike them, too, in modern English sex and gender nearly always correspond. But not only are there exceptions to this but other traps too, and the matter requires considerable vigilance, as we shall see in Chapter Five.

---

10 **NB** It follows that no structure lacking a finite verb qualifies as a sentence, an important point to bear in mind when engaged on formal writing.

12 Gerund

The Gerund is a *verbal noun* ending in **-ing**. That, I have found, is a difficult concept for many students to grasp, partly because many other words ending in **-ing** either form part of a finite verb –

They **were running** away   He **is writing** an essay

– or function as adjectives:

the *gurgling* drain   a *refreshing* drink

It is hardly surprising, therefore, that people find it very hard to imagine that a word ending in **-ing** can function as a **noun**. But that is what is happening in these three sentences:

1 **Eating prawns is one of life's pleasures.**
2 **They like playing football.**
3 **She bought some new bedding.**

In each example there is already a finite verb: *is, like and bought*. In the first one the **-ing** word is the verb's subject – *eating* **is** – and in the others its object – **like** *playing,* **bought** . . . *bedding*. In all three instances the sentences could be recast to emphasise more obviously the -ing words' noun-status:

1a *The eating of* prawns is one of life's pleasures.
2a They like *the playing of* football.
3a She bought some new bed*clothes*.

1a and 2a are admittedly clumsy, but although they are stylistically inferior to 1 and 2, the new presence of **the** helps confirm that *eating* and *playing* are nouns; in 3a the substitution of the more 'normal' noun *bedclothes* does the same job.

13 Impersonal verb

Despite the grand title, this is a simple matter. If the formal definition

A verb in which the source of the action is not indicated

seems rather a mouthful, in practice it boils down to the use of **it** as the subject of the verb:

It is raining   It's a pity   It was a surprise

14 The simple infinitive

In essence, the infinitive is the root form of a verb from which grow all other forms. It is not **defined** by a subject or made **finite** by being placed in time: hence *infinitive*. In its classic form the English infinitive is preceded by the word 'to':

to behave; to eat; to die; to desire; to mow; to kiss.

In practice, the 'to' is not always used. Look at these two linked examples:

1a I ought *to go* now.   1b I should *go* now.

They mean the same thing; in each case **go** is an infinitive. It's simply that in certain instances English usage over the years has led to the dropping of the 'to'.[11]

15 Mood

Mood is the form of a verb which shows the mode or manner in which a statement is made. There are four moods:

The indicative mood Used when a statement is made as a fact
She is a teacher
or a question
What are you doing?
or an exclamation
What a performance!
or as a supposition regarded as a fact
If he refuses, and he certainly will refuse, nothing can be done.
The imperative mood Used to express a command
Go away Drink up
See also **ellipsis** above.

11 The rather more complicated **perfect infinitive** is covered in the next chapter.

The subjunctive mood   Used to express a wish, purpose, or
                       condition. The point – and value – of
                       the subjunctive is that its use implies an
                       unlikely or indeed impossible
                       supposition, as in probably the
                       commonest subjunctive in English:
                       If I *were* you . . .

The infinitive mood   The root form of a verb, undefined by
                       either subject or tense. See also **infinitive**
                       above.

16   Transitive and intransitive use of verbs

A verb is used **transitively** when it expresses an action exercised by the
doer upon some object:

He paddled his own *canoe*.

A verb is used **intransitively** when it expresses an action which is
confined to the doer:

After an exhausting day at the office *he slept* like a baby.

This matter is a complicated one, in that many verbs can be either
transitive or intranstive according to use and context. We return to it
early in the next chapter.

That concludes our preliminary guide, which I hope has proved
helpful. However, unless you're already very well schooled in all the
matters it addressed,[12] you will probably require further instruction
and assistance. With that in mind, Section 1.3 is a kind of sketch map
of what the succeeding chapters now offer.

1.3   GRAMMAR: AN OUTLINE MENU

It is highly unlikely that all readers of this book will have identical needs.
Some may be comfortable about the various parts of speech but
experience difficulty with any kind of syntactical analysis; some may be

12 In that case it's most unlikely you need this book at all!

entirely sound apart from the odd confusion or blind spot; some may be beginners. I've divided the material accordingly, allowing you to skip the bits you don't need, or to go first to the section where you need most help.

Number	Chapter Title	Focus
2	**Parts of speech**	The jobs words do
3	**Inflections**	Changes in the form of words according to the job they are doing
4	**Syntax**	How words operate in groups, as parts of sentences
5	**Parts of speech II (advanced)**	A further, more sophisticated look at the jobs words do. Includes clause analysis and an indexed glossary of terms.
6	**Punctuation: speech and quotation**	
7	**Additional gaps and traps**	A miscellany of specific items that cause trouble to many.

Regular practice exercises are included throughout; you might like to try Exercise 2, which revisits some of the terms and points covered during this introductory chapter.

Exercise 2 *A revision miscellany*

A The following sentences contain at least one error in usage, agreement, number or word order. Can you identify them?

1 The traffic warden was in an unpleasantly masterly mood.
2 As a snake, he found the green mamba unexpectedly beautiful.
3 She switched jobs in order to work less hours.
4 'I wish you wouldn't behave like that Philip,' she complained.
5 There were no cauliflower's on sale and no fish neither.

B In these **complex sentences**, which is the **main clause** and which the **subordinate clause**?

6 If at first you don't succeed, try again.
7 I won't go out until I've heard from you.

---

continued

8   Since you're determined to go through with this, I'll shut up.
9   Whenever I hear the word 'salad' my spirits droop.
10   It might be better to give up once you've failed three times.
11   As he walked through the door, his dog leapt up in welcome.

C What is the **mood** of these sentences – **indicative, imperative** or **subjunctive**?

12   How much is that doggy in the window?
13   He was overjoyed to see her looking so well.
14   Get out of here this minute!
15   Were he to do that, he'd be very unwise.
16   I've never seen anything like it!
17   Please put that book down.

D Which of these words ending in **-ing** is a **gerund**, which is an **adjective**, and which is part of a **verb**?

18   There was no spare clothing and no running water.
19   Cycling is growing in popularity
20   They were playing a particularly absorbing game of chess.

Answers are in Appendix II.

Chapter 2

Parts of speech

2.1 PRELIMINARY

It should be stressed at once that

A Part of Speech does not define a word exhaustively; it merely describes its current function.

The distinction is important, because a host of English words can operate as several different parts of speech, depending on the circumstances of their use.

Take for example two very common words, **table** and **fast**.

Most people would say that 'table' is a noun and that 'fast' is an adjective; they would be quite right, as these simple sentences illustrate:

1   The table is brown, rectangular and polished.
2   He caught a fast train to London.

However, table can also be used as an adjective or as a verb:

3   She bought a beautifully   Here **table**, like 'beautifully
    carved table lamp.   carved', describes the lamp

4   The MP for Derby tabled   Here **tabled** denotes an action,
    a motion in the Commons.   something done.

Similarly, **fast** can have other functions – an adverb:

5   She ran fast   Here **fast** modifies (gives more information
                          about) the verb 'ran', telling us how she
                          performed the action.

It can also be a noun:

6   The pilgrims observed a twenty-four hour fast in recognition of those starving in the Third World.

And a verb:

7   Jesus fasted for forty days and forty nights.

Those seven examples are I trust clear enough when examined. But that is the point: very often one cannot tell what part of speech a word is unless its context is closely examined.

Words are as versatile as certain more concrete objects. One can buy all-purpose cleaning substances that are just as effective for wood as they are for metals, glass, linoleum or fabrics. Many foodstuffs are similarly versatile. Vegetables can be used to complement meat or fish; they can be the central constituent of a dish (as in all vegetarian cooking); they can be primarily decorative; they can be adjuncts for dips or soups, and so on. In each case, the cleaning substance or the vegetable has its function adjusted according to the needs and wishes of the user. Words work in a very similar way; indeed, there may be occasions when one legitimately *invents* a new function for a word, as did Ted Hughes in the opening stanza to his poem 'Pike', where he uses 'tiger' as a verb. In terms of formal grammar, there is no such verb as 'to tiger'. But Hughes's daring invention is totally successful: his use of 'tigering' suggests both the colouring of the fish and its innate ferocity, which is followed up in the next line. Such linguistic suppleness and imagination are founded on an alert sense of the work words do and can be made to do.

THE EIGHT PARTS OF SPEECH

Verb	A word (or group of words) used to denote actions, states or happenings.
Noun	A word used to name something.
Adjective	A word that qualifies (describes) a noun.
Adverb	A word used to modify (tell us more about) a verb, an adjective or another adverb.
Conjunction	A word used to connect one part of a sentence to another.
Preposition	A word placed before another word to locate the latter in time or space.

Pronoun   A word used to stand for a noun.
Interjection   A word used to express mood or reaction.

You may acquire a clearer idea of these terms if we group them thus:

GROUP A	GROUP B	GROUP C	MAVERICK
Noun	Verb	Conjunction	Interjection
Pronoun	Adverb	Preposition	
Adjective			

Group A   consists of words which name things or give more information about the things so named.

Group B   consists of words that denote actions, states and happenings and words that describe those actions, states and happenings.

Group C   consists of words that connect or pin down other words or groups of words.

Maverick   simply means odd one out. Interjections have no grammatical connection with the rest of a sentence.

The rest of the chapter is devoted to a detailed look at each term.

2.2 VERBS: AN INTRODUCTION

Most surveys of Parts of Speech begin with the noun and the adjective. I have placed the verb first because it is the most important part of any sentence. In addition, I'm convinced that once you understand the various forms and functions of the verb, all other Parts of Speech will be easier to comprehend.

Forty years ago verbs were often referred to by primary teachers as 'doing words'. A lot of people came to sneer at this, pointing out that many verbs do not denote any 'doing' at all – every verb of being and becoming, for instance. But while the term had its shortcomings, it is much more helpful than subsequent alternatives such as 'process words' or 'active signifiers'. If you are even occasionally unsure which part of a sentence is the verb, this description may help:

In any sentence, the verb is the word or words which tells you what is happening, whether it be an action (something *done*) or a state of being (something *felt* or just something *existing*).

Here are three simple examples.

1   The boy kicked the ball.
2   His strength surprised him.
3   The ball landed over a hundred yards away.

In Sentence 1, **kicked** is, evidently enough, a physical action – a genuine 'doing word', if you like!

In Sentence 2, **surprised** is not an action as such; but it still tells us what happened – in this case that a powerful feeling affected the boy.

In Sentence 3, **landed** again tells us what happened – in this case a statement concerning the ball's destination.

Now try the elementary exercise below.

Exercise 3

Identify the verb in these sentences. 1–7 are 'simple' (i.e. one-word) verbs; 8–10 are compounds (two or more words).

1   The anxious householder telephoned the police.
2   The wind's strength appalled him.
3   Hitler was arguably the twentieth century's most evil genius.
4   Lightning destroyed the chapel.
5   To everyone's surprise she became the school's best cricketer.
6   The chef cautiously tasted the soup.
7   The kitten savaged the ball of wool.
8   No one has ever vanquished death.
9   She will be returning shortly.
10   This result will disappoint him greatly.

Answers are in Appendix II.

Next, a detailed exploration of something touched on briefly in the previous chapter.

Transitive and intransitive verbs

In any sentence, a verb is either **transitive** or **intransitive**.

Transitive means 'passing across': if you think of **transfer, transmitter** or **Trans-Atlantic**, you'll get the general idea. If a verb is transitive, it means that the action passes from the 'do-er' (the **subject**) across to something or someone else (the **object**).
For example:

1   The police **captured** the fugitive.
2   The ball **smashed** the window.

In each case there is a transfer of action. **The fugitive** and **the window** are on the direct receiving end of actions by **the police** and **the ball**. So the verbs are **transitive**.
Intransitive simply means 'not transitive': there is no 'passing across'. The action of an intransitive verb refers solely to the **subject**.
For example:

3   The lion **roared**.
4   The tide **receded**.

Those are complete sentences making complete sense. Nothing other than the subject (**lion, tide**) is affected or even implied.
As you'll gather, identifying a verb as transitive or intransitive involves working out what is happening and whether anyone or anything else is involved. It is important to be able to do this, because many English verbs can be **either** transitive **or** intransitive, depending on how they are used.
Take the verb **run**, for instance. Most commonly it is a verb of motion, and as such it is intransitive.

5   You **run** exceptionally fast.
6   They **ran** down the street.

No 'transfer of action' occurs. In 6, **down the street** is a phrase telling you *where* the action took place: it is an adverb.

But take a look at this sentence:

7   The car **ran down** the pedestrian.

This is transitive. The word **down** belongs to **ran** rather than to **the pedestrian**, forming a compound verb that means 'rammed'.
These uses are transitive also:

8   She **runs** her own business.
9   The huntsmen **ran** the fox five miles.

Both involve a 'passing across': 8 means that the woman **manages** a commercial enterprise, 9 that the huntsmen **chased** the fox for a distance of five miles. Each verb has a direct impact on a separate thing or creature, and thus is transitive.

It might help you to remember that

A   **All sentences have a subject and a verb.**
B   **Only sentences whose verb is transitive have an *object*.**

Now try the brief exercise that follows.

Exercise 4

Pick out **subject, verb** and, *if there is one*, **object** in these sentences.

1   The bomb destroyed the house.
2   The dog bit the postman.
3   Then the postman bit the dog.
4   The man walked as if crippled.
5   The children walked the dog.
6   The cheetah ran over the field.
7   The lecturer ran over the main ideas.
8   The bulldozer ran over the hedgehog.

Answers are in Appendix II.

The infinitive

We looked in Chapter One at the **simple infinitive** as the most basic form of every verb; we shall also be returning to it in Chapter Five. Here we need to look at its slightly more complex incarnation, the **perfect infinitive**.[1]

---

1   To understand **perfect** as a grammatical term, you need to forget about 'excellent', 'unimprovable' or any such apparent synonym. It is most commonly taken to be an alternative to 'past' as a descriptor of **tense**, and that is indeed its application in this current instance. But its broader and more strictly accurate grammatical signification is 'fully realised' or 'completed', which helps explain why there are also **present perfect** and **future perfect** tenses. This whole area is covered shortly: see pp. 29–31.

On the surface, there's nothing too tricky about this concept. It may be less raw than its **simple** colleague in that it is removed in time –

to have lived; to have eaten; to have betrayed.

– but while those structures indicate the past, they remain root forms, undefined by subject or context.

However, the **perfect infinitive** can all too easily lead the writer into murky waters. Look at these sentences:

1   **He would have liked to have stayed.**
2   **They intended to have left the country last month.**
3   **She seemed to have disgraced herself at the dance.**

She seemed to have disgraced herself at the dance.

All three are bloated; 2 and 3 are additionally ambiguous.

One's main verb is already perfect – **would have liked** – so the sequent perfect (**to have stayed**) is clumsy, indeed tautologous.[2] It should be written as

> **He would have liked *to stay*.**

In 2 the simple infinitive **to leave** is also much better, avoiding both clumsiness and confusion. For if left as it stands, it is possible to interpret 2 as

> **They intended to have left the country *by* last month.**

A similar awkwardness and also a lack of clarity attend 3, which could signify that she arrived at the dance *already* disgraced. Better to write either –

> **She seems to have disgraced herself at the dance.**
> or
> **She seemed to disgrace herself at the dance.**

– both of which are correct.

All infinitives, whether simple or perfect, are the undeveloped form of the verb; to develop them one needs to select person, number and tense.

Person and number

All verbs can be placed in one of three **persons** (1st, 2nd, 3rd) and one of two **numbers** (singular, plural). Taking as models the two infinitives **to drive** and **to mend**, the full list, or *conjugation*, runs:

1	First person singular	**I drive**
		I mend

---

2 A **tautology** is a phrase where at least one word is redundant. Comically obvious examples include 'spineless invertebrate', 'new innovation' and (my favourite) 'dead corpse'. Cynics or wags might propose that such structures as 'appalling rail system', 'unreliable pension scheme' and 'crap daytime television' are equally tautologous, in the UK if nowhere else.

2	Second person singular	**you drive**
		you mend
3	Third person singular	**he/she/one/it drives**
		he/she/one/it mends
4	First person plural	**we drive**
		we mend
5	Second person plural	**you drive**
		you mend
6	Third person plural	**they drive**
		they mend

Both models are called **regular** verbs, which are relatively straightforward in English, unlike several other languages. In addition, however, English has several hundred **irregular** verbs – that is, verbs that deviate from the forms defined by **drive** and **mend**. One such verb is to be, the commonest and most fundamental verb of all:

1   **I am**
2   **You are**
3   **He/she/one/it is**
4   **We are**
5   **You are**
6   **They are**

Generally speaking, person and number only present problems when questions of grammatical agreement arise. This matter is covered in Chapter Four, which also includes a further, more extensive study of irregular verbs.

Tense

In essence, **tense** means 'time': a verb's tense establishes the time in which it is set. There are three main tenses:

past	present	future
I ate	I eat	I shall eat

Each of these main tenses can have modifications. The form of these depends on whether the action is *complete* (known grammatically as a **perfect** tense) or *incomplete*, part of a process still in operation (known as **imperfect** or **continuous** tenses).

Thus:

A	I ate	are past tenses in the **perfect** form.
	I **have eaten**	
B	I **was eating**	is the **past imperfect** or **past continuous**.
C	I eat	is the present tense in the **perfect** form.
D	I **am eating**	is the **continuous present**, alternatively known as the **present imperfect**.
E	I **shall eat**	is the future tense in the **perfect** form.
F	I **shall be eating**	is the **future continuous**, alternatively called the **future imperfect**.

Finally, there are two other tenses, more complex than the rest.

G   The **pluperfect**   is a past tense one stage further removed in
time:
I **had eaten**

Its value lies in allowing a writer to distinguish between different times
in the past:

(a)   (b)
After I had eaten,   there was a sudden explosion.

In that little narrative sequence, it is clear that Event (a) occurred **before**
Event (b). And while a term like **pluperfect** may seem intimidating and
confusing, if you are alert to its function, it can give your writing valuable
increased range.

H   The **future perfect**   looks forward to a time when a proposed
action or event has been duly completed.

By the time you've finished shopping, I **shall have eaten**.

As with the pluperfect, this tense affords you greatly increased range in
your writing and speech, allowing you to establish time zones that are
more subtle and precise than those offered by basic past, present and
future tenses.

Note: This section has been introductory rather than comprehensive.
Additional tenses – for example, the conditional and the future in the

past – are studied on pp 80–94, which also explains other complex matters, including how to translate tenses from direct speech into reported speech.

Voice

Verbs are cast in one of two voices: **active** or **passive**. The choice depends on whether you wish the subject to **act** or **be acted upon**. That rather ponderous explanation is best amplified by some examples.

1   The audience cheered the conductor with wild enthusiasm.
2   The union fined the man £100.
3   Lightning destroyed the chapel.

Those sentences all have **active** verbs. The subjects (**audience, union, lightning**) are in charge of the relevant actions (**cheered, fined, destroyed**). The other nouns mentioned (**conductor, man, chapel**) are directly on the receiving end of those actions.

Supposing, however, you want to redesign those sentences and place the **object** first. You cannot do this simply by switching the position of the nouns in question: that would utterly transform the meaning.

1a   The conductor cheered the audience with wild enthusiasm.
2a   The man fined the union £100.
3a   The chapel destroyed lightning.

1a and 2a still make sense, although their information is so surprising as to become almost comic. 3a is of course absurd.

So merely reversing the position of the words is no good, because you reverse the meaning as well. But you can place **conductor / man / chapel** at the head of the sentence, *provided you alter the form of the verb*:

1b   The conductor **was cheered by** the audience with wild enthusiasm.
2b   The man **was fined** £100 **by** the union.
3b   The chapel **was destroyed by** lightning.

The verbs have been recast in the **passive voice**. Grammatically speaking, what has happened is that words that were originally the **object** of actions have become the **subject** that is **acted upon**. There is no significant change in meaning; there is an observable difference in emphasis.

Passives should be used infrequently. You ought normally to use the **active** voice: it is simpler, more direct, more efficient. But there are times when the passive is the better choice, for reasons of emphasis. Let us take a last look at the three sentences we've been using.

In 1, it makes little difference in emphasis whether you choose active or passive. Therefore the active form is better. But in 2 and 3 there is a genuine difference. If you choose the active voice –

> The union fined the man £100.
> Lightning destroyed the chapel.

– you give the star role or major emphasis to the two subjects (**union, lightning**). That does not mean that **the man** or **the chapel** are unimportant or uninteresting, but it does mean that the reader's strongest visual attention is focused on the thing carrying out the action. However, if you wish instead to fix that attention on **the man** or **the chapel**, you need to introduce that focus at once, and the passive voice becomes your better choice:

> The man was fined £100 by the union.
> The chapel was destroyed by lightning.

People sometimes use the passive voice to soften the impact of an order, especially in business letters. Look at these two pairs of examples:

4a   You should send us a cheque in payment immediately.
4b   A cheque should be sent in payment immediately.
5a   I would appreciate an early reply.
5b   An early reply would be appreciated.

It could be argued that 4a and 5a are somewhat hectoring, even threatening, and that 4b and 5b are therefore safer and more courteous structures. Well, yes; but it could also be argued that 4b and 5b are simply timid, wrapping up a direct requirement in a needlessly elaborate, fudging way. It all depends on how urgent the writer considers the matter to be, or even how annoyed s/he is! If 4a's firm really needs that cheque, or has been waiting an unreasonably long time for it, the added pressure that the active voice embodies is fully justified; similarly, if the writer of 5a is thoroughly fed up with having letters ignored, that is the right choice rather than 5b.

Such tonal matters are important, and you must be the judge of them when you write.[3] In general, though, I suggest trying to limit your use of

---

3   And don't be bullied by Grammar Check software!

the passive to those times when emphasis is the criterion. To use it to soften or dilute may seem sensible, but it's worth bearing in mind that

Writing that hedges its bets, is worried or simply scared, will invariably be bad writing.

Calling a spade a spade need not cause offence or become impolite. On the contrary, many readers will thank you for making things as clear and direct as you can.

The terms **active** and **passive** are hardly fascinating in and of themselves, and even a full understanding of their function is not of much use on its own. But I hope you can see from this section that such an understanding plus the always-crucial facility to think clearly about the effect you wish to make add up to a most valuable tool. Grammatical terms may seem arid as words on a page, but a sharp sense of how they can be used will quickly lead to a significant improvement in your writing and powers of expression. The same goes for the next topic – the **mood** of a verb.

Mood

Verbs are placed in one of three moods: **indicative, imperative** and **subjunctive**. Once again, these are tricky-looking terms, but in practice only the last is at all problematic.

Most of the verbs we use are in the **indicative** mood, which is employed when we make statements or ask questions.

1 **She drives me crazy.**
2 **Why are you bothering with a tablecloth? They're all so drunk that they won't even notice.**
3 **He disappeared one day, and nobody understood why.**
4 **What are you talking about?**

All seven verbs in that collection are in the **indicative** mood. They **indicate** information, or the desire for information, in a straightfoward, unqualified fashion.

The **imperative** mood is used for commands or entreaties.

5 **Stop the car.**
6 **Give me your badge.**
7 **Please don't forget to write.**

As you may recall from the previous chapter, the imperative is easily recognised: the subject (**you**) is rarely included, being 'understood'.

There is also a first person plural imperative, which is as much a suggestion as a command:

8 **Let's go.**
9 **Let us pray.**
10 **Let's play Scrabble.**

The **subjunctive** is regularly found in Latin, French and German, but its use in English is rare. It is important nonetheless, because it is used in remarks where supposition or condition are implied, and thus it can play a subtle part in establishing precise meaning.

In the previous chapter I commented that the expression

11 **If I were you . . .**

is probably the commonest subjunctive in English. It is, obviously, impossible for anyone to be someone else: when we use this popular expression, we are imagining what we would do if we found ourselves in that other person's position. The advice that we give may well be valuable, but it is wholly suppositional, and the subjunctive telegraphs that fact.

Sometimes the use of the subjunctive is more delicate in terms of meaning. Consider this pair of sentences:

12a **If James gives up smoking, he'll be fit in no time.**
12b **If James were to give up smoking, he'd be fit in no time.**

On the surface, they say the same thing. But 12a is, don't you find, more positive than 12b? The speaker seems to be fairly confident that James *will* give up smoking. In 12b, however, the tonal implication is that James won't give up smoking, or that he is unlikely to do so. By casting the remark in the **subjunctive** mood, 12b suggests a lack of confidence in James's willingness or willpower.

The subjunctive resembles the passive, in that it is a neat way of altering tone and impact. Used with that precise aim in mind, it is a vital part of a writer's armoury; it is also important to be able to recognise its use by others, in order to judge their tone correctly. But just as you should usually stick to the active voice, you'll find that most of your verbs are indicative ones. If the subjunctive occurs in your writing more than

occasionally, you're probably hedging your bets too much or are not sufficiently certain of what you think or want to say.

Auxiliary verbs

An **auxiliary** means a 'helper' or a 'secondary aid'. **Auxiliary verbs** are used to help another verb form one of its tenses, moods or voices. There have been many examples in this section already – for instance, all those verbs listed under **imperfect** or **continuous** tense forms.

Altogether there are sixteen such verbs. Three are **primary** –

be   do   have

used to form compounds of ordinary verbs:

1   I **am** going to London.
2   I **do** not think that is true.
3   I **have** been for a long walk.

The other thirteen are **modal** – that is, they express grammatical mood or, to an extent, tense.

4   I **shall** resign tomorrow.
5   It looks as if it **may** rain.

Modal auxiliaries are examined in detail in Chapter Five. The full list is:

can	must	should
could	need	used (to)
dare	ought (to)	will
may	shall	would
might		

Participles

There are two kinds of participle:

The past participle is usually formed by adding **-d** or **-ed** to the infinitive:

decided   denoted   departed   discussed

There are however a sizeable number of exceptions – for example:

sung   brought   been   had   run   learnt

I'm afraid there is no 'rule' I can offer to guide you through such irregularities: they just have to be learnt (!) one at a time.[4]
The past participle combines with an auxiliary verb to form a past tense:

1   I have decided.
2   They had departed three hours earlier.
3   Why haven't you brought your pyjamas?
4   She was run off her feet.

The past participle also has a separate function as a simple adjective: this is examined on p. 52.

The present participle always ends in -ing. It combines with an auxiliary verb to form a continuous tense:

5   In a few hours, thank God, I shall be **sleeping**.
6   They were **waiting** patiently in the bitter cold.
7   If I were **writing** this in longhand, I'd go mad.

Like the past participle, the present participle has a separate life as an adjective. Again, you will find this covered on pp. 100–3.[5]

That concludes our preliminary look at the verb. As you'll gather from the occasional references to Chapter Five, there is much more to say and know about the work verbs can do and the form they can take. But if you've understood all the material in this section, you should now have a sound grasp of this most central part of speech, and as a result I'm confident that you'll find the rest of this chapter progressively more comfortable to master. The **verb** is the most complex, the most far-

---

4   The case of **learnt** (past participle of learn) is complicated by the fact that there is a word **learned**. It is an adjective meaning 'well read, erudite' and is pronounced with two syllables: **learn-ed**.
5   *Warning*: words ending in -ing are not necessarily **present participles**. One of the commonest words in English, *thing*, is a **common noun**; in addition there is the **gerund**, which is a verbal noun that also takes the -ing ending. See above, Chapter One, p. 16 and also below, Chapter Five, pp. 100–3.

reaching and the most muscular device in language, compared to which all other parts of speech will, I trust, seem straightforward. Before we move onto **nouns**, therefore, try the exercises on the next two pages, which test all the material so far. If you can score well on them, you should have little fear of anything else that grammar can throw at you!

Exercise 5

A Pick out the verbs in these sentences and identify which of them are **transitive**, and which **intransitive**.

1 The sun was shining.
2 The sun burnt the grass.
3 The word-processor exploded.
4 He bought a new word-processor.
5 The tennis coach hit the ball very hard.
6 This record will be a big hit.

B Put these sentences into the **tense** designated.

1	I go to the shops.	(continuous present)
2	The floods were devastating.	(pluperfect)
3	They appear on 'Big Brother'.	(past imperfect)
4	He passed his driving test.	(future perfect)
5	Julian sees Susan every day.	(future continuous)

C What **mood** (indicative, imperative or subjunctive) are these sentences in?

1 How are you?
2 Put yourself in my place.
3 I'd be amazed if that were to happen.
4 I'll be happy if that happens.
5 Please make an effort this time.
6 Let's have a party.

Answers are in Appendix II.

Exercise 6

A Change these sentences from the **active** to the **passive voice**.

1 The snake swallowed the bird.
2 The gale blew the slates off the roof.
3 The band did not satisfy the large audience.

B Change these sentences from the **passive** to the **active voice**.

1 An early settlement of your account would be appreciated.
2 The charity's funds were embezzled by the treasurer.
3 All travel arrangements have been taken care of by your Sunshine Tours representative.

C Provide the correct **past participle** of the verb given in brackets to make the sentence grammatically accurate.

1 Have you (bring) the flowers?
2 She had (commit) herself to three years' work.
3 Where has my car (go)?
4 He had (hop) off the field, nursing his injured foot.
5 I have (cut) my finger badly.

D What's the difference in **meaning** or **effect** between these two pairs of sentences?

1a The organisation was destroyed by its own inner corruption.
1b Its own inner corruption destroyed the organisation.
2a If you do that, you'll regret it.
2b If you were to do that, you'd regret it.

Answers are in Appendix II.

2.3 NOUNS

There are four types of noun:

1 **Common** or **concrete**

2   **Proper**
3   **Collective**
4   **Abstract**

Over thirty years ago, just as verbs were often called 'doing words', so nouns were referred to as 'naming words'. This primary-school term was useful when thinking about types 1–3 but far less successful when type 4 was under consideration. Nouns do 'name' things, yes; it is nevertheless forgivably hard for pupils to regard such words as **grace, happiness, misery** or **stupidity** (all abstract nouns) as 'things'. So if the concept noun does not yet make complete sense to you, a better way of defining and identifying all kinds of noun is needed. We can best do this by looking in turn at each type.

Common or concrete nouns⁶

Let's start with some examples.

millionaire   earthquake   comet   rhinoceros   lord   silk

Those six words are all common nouns, but the term is useless (or worse) unless its exact meaning is understood:

> **Common here has nothing to do with *ordinariness, frequent occurrence* or *vulgarity.***

Millionaires and **earthquakes** are hardly ordinary; **comets** are not an everyday phenomenon and the **rhinoceros** is threatened with extinction; **silk** is far from being 'cheap and nasty', nor is a **lord** likely to be 'common as muck'.

Common can also denote 'belonging equally to', and that is the meaning that applies here.

---

6   Grammarians would argue that in suggesting that **common noun** and **concrete noun** are synonymous I am conflating two quite separate terms. They would be perfectly correct in doing so and I address the matter in Chapter Five. At this stage, however, I am concerned with assisting anyone who is unclear about this most basic of nouns and what differentiates it from other types, especially the **abstract noun**. My procedure here may be unorthodox, but it is designed to clarify and make comfortable a concept that many students find difficult and confusing. Those who already have a sound understanding can afford to skip this section and consult instead the more sophisticated later explanations.

> A common noun is the name common to all members of or items in the class named by the noun.

That is a good, precise definition,[7] but I still don't like it much – mainly because I don't care for the term itself. In my experience it confuses rather than illuminates, and I much prefer the term **concrete noun**.

Concrete means 'physically substantial' or 'existing in material form'. A **concrete noun** is one that can be apprehended by the senses – any, several or all of them. This point is very important when it comes to deciding what an **abstract noun** is, as we'll see shortly.

Some further examples:

man   desk   ashtray   leopard   pump   book

All are **concrete**. We identify these things through our senses: they have physical properties. And all are **common**: each one signals a set of characteristics that define all men, all desks and so forth. Of course, individuals can and will vary greatly: men can be short or tall, good or evil, black or white and a host of other things; desks can be metal or wooden, bare or cluttered, and so on. But the nouns make immediate sense to us because they produce a standard image in our minds, one which identifies the essence of a man, a desk, so forth. That is what **common** in the grammatical sense really means, and it is easier to visualise that essence because of its **concreteness**.

Proper nouns

Proper nouns always begin with a capital letter. They name a particular person, thing or place. For example:

1   **Mario** is a **Catholic**. He is a trainee priest at **St Peter's** in **Rome**. He used to be engaged to **Julietta**, but had to renounce marriage when he entered the **Church**.

Notice that the words **Catholic** and **Church**, capitalised here, could in other circumstances be correctly spelt with a small c. **Catholic** is always capitalised when its reference is to the Church of Rome, but it takes a small c when used as an adjective meaning broad-minded or wide-ranging, as in:

---

7   Furnished by S. H. Burton, *Mastering English Language*, p. 131.

2   His tastes in music are remarkably catholic: he has an equal enthusiasm for **Puccini, Oscar Peterson** and **Pink Floyd.**

Similarly, **Church** is only capitalised when it refers to an ecclesiastical body. Look at these two sentences:

3   He entered the church.
4   He entered the Church.

The only visible difference is the lower/upper case **c**; the difference in meaning is nevertheless considerable.

Sentence 3 means that an unspecified male stepped inside a building designed for and symbolising religious worship. It could be any such building, anywhere in the world, and he could be entering it for any reason – to pray, to attend a service, to change the flowers, to rob the collection box, so forth.

Sentence 4 is much more specific, telling us that an adult man took Holy Orders: he committed himself to becoming a priest of some kind (the meaning in Sentence 1).

Those four examples make a point that has a broader significance than the consideration of **proper nouns.** They show that tiny differences in the visual presentation of words can make a major difference to their meaning. This is a good place to stress the matter nonetheless, because capitalisation – the obvious hallmark of a proper noun – is a device that can on its own radically change the function of a word, and that's why it is important that you learn to recognise what proper nouns are and to spell all of them correctly.

Collective nouns

A **collective noun** names a group or collection of things, persons or creatures. Such nouns are easy to recognise because they are always followed by, or imply, the word **of:**

a herd of cattle   **a bunch of daffodils**   **a class of students**

The collective noun is singular in **grammatical number** even though it stands for a plural aggregate, and must therefore be used with a singular verb. This may seem obvious enough, but it can easily be forgotten when using words like **army, library or galaxy**, whose 'members' may add up to millions.

Incidentally, one of the most delightful aspects of English is its taste for the exotic when deciding upon collectives. Do you know these?

a **charm** of goldfinches   a **murmuration** of starlings
a **school** of porpoises   a **whoop** of gorillas

A whoop of gorillas.

Abstract nouns

Abstract nouns name qualities, feelings, notions – anything strictly non-physical. I stress 'strictly' because a large number of people err in this area, perhaps because they've been taught this popular formula:

If you cannot see it, hear it or touch it, it's abstract.

This works most of the time: ultimately it won't do. I once had an argument with a fellow-teacher about the status of the word **air**. She maintained – observing that formula – that **air** is abstract. Was she correct?

Well, you cannot **see** air, you cannot **hear** it (unless and until it becomes **wind**, which is a separate concept) and you certainly cannot **touch** it, as anyone who has tried to grab a handful of air will confirm. The fact remains that if air were an abstract noun, we'd all be dead: indeed, no human, animal or plant could ever have survived for more than thirty seconds! Air contains life-giving oxygen and a host of other gases, and is basic to all existence.[8] In view of this, one could argue that **air** is *the* most fundamental **concrete** noun of all.

The above formula is thus inadequate, and needs replacing with something more comprehensive and precise:

> **An abstract noun names something devoid of all physical properties and which can only be apprehended by the mind rather than through any of the five senses.**

Of course, **all** words are inventions: they have evolved through human thought and humans' need to signify things to other humans. **Concrete** nouns are straightforward inventions, in that they do not often promote argument or misunderstanding. Words like **table, banana, dustbin, television** or **water** are unlikely to cause problems between any two people competent in English. But **abstract** nouns are more intricate: they are *doubly* inventions. They perform not only the creative act of naming, but also the creation of a non-material concept. That is why they seem – often *are* – harder to understand than other types of noun, and it's also why they can cause so much confusion.

Take the abstract noun **morality**, for example. Now I might be completely confident that I understand its meaning; but you might have a very different understanding. We'd soon find that any discussion we might have on the subject would either become very difficult to pursue or simply break down; at the heart of an exchange of views conducted in a language apparently common to us both would lie two separate and probably conflicting ideas of what **morality** means. Such occasions are frustrating enough: just imagine what life would be like if all words were as slippery. Suppose that every time I used the word **tree**, some of my audience imagined I meant **lawnmower**, some **umbrella**, some

---

8   In the same way, all gases are concrete nouns, even if our physical awareness of them is infrequent.

handkerchief and others **avocado**. Communication would be impossible, life absurd.

On the other hand, potential ambiguity and elusiveness make abstract nouns interesting as well as difficult. This is as it should be: they are ideas, and ideas interest most people. Few would find such words as **umbrella**, **handkerchief** or **desk** endlessly invigorating in and of themselves; but concepts like **grace, happiness, oppression** and **politics** have fascinated men and women since civilisation began.

This brief detour into the philosophy and practice of language may not seem to have a close bearing on functional grammar; it nevertheless has emphasised the need for clarity and successful communication. The more you are aware of the problems (and benefits) that attend abstract nouns, the better your grasp and use of English will be.

Noun phrases and noun clauses

I've so far concentrated on nouns as single words. But a phrase or clause can also fulfil the function of a noun, as in these four examples.

1   **Starting the race** is no problem: the finish bothers me a lot.
2   The entire assignment depends on your **ability to enter the building unnoticed**.
3   Tell me **what you were doing**.
4   According to **what we hear**, there is no evidence against him.

In each case, the highlighted words combine to perform a single function – that of a noun.

In 1, you might think that **starting** the race is a verb; notice, however, that the phrase **starting the race** could be replaced by the simple noun **The start** without any real change in meaning and no change in grammatical function: both choices form the subject of the verb is.[9]

In 2, all the highlighted words are dependent on the preposition on. Prepositions can only govern nouns or pronouns; since the structure is not a pronoun, it must be a noun. Again, the phrase could be replaced by a single-word noun, even if such a substitution would make for a less precise statement:

2a   The entire assignment depends on your **invisibility**.

---

9   **Starting the race** here is another example of the **gerund**.

In 3, **what you were doing** is the **object** of the verb **Tell**. It is a clause, not a phrase, since it includes a finite verb, but otherwise it is just like 1 and 2 in fulfilling the function of a noun. As in those two, the clause could be replaced by a simple noun plus a preceding adjective.

3a   Tell me your **actions**.

In 4, as in 2, the highlighted words are dependent on a preposition – **according to**. As in 3, we have a clause here, not a phrase, because of the finite verb **we hear**. But the function is again that of a noun, as this single-word noun replacement shows.

4a   According to **rumour**, there is no evidence against him.

That concludes this preliminary look at nouns. For more sophisticated examination of the types of noun described above, please consult Chapter Five. In the meantime, try this exercise.

Exercise 7

A Ten nouns follow. Identify each one as common/concrete, proper, collective or abstract.

1	hearth	6	flock
2	Belgrade	7	cigarette
3	army	8	Caesar
4	misery	9	ink
5	depression	10	gravity

B In this passage there are four concrete/common nouns, three proper nouns, two collective nouns and three abstract nouns. Can you find them all?

The man looked with indifference at the vast gathering of eagles landing on Big Ben. A fleet of traffic, including countless buses and taxis, had stopped in Parliament Square to watch in fascination; but his only interest lay in finding the nearest McDonald's and buying a huge hamburger.

continued

C Pick out the noun phrases (1–3) and noun clauses (4–6) in these sentences.

1   Catching the last train home always tires me out.
2   The old man's delight in painting was infectious.
3   Can you tell me the name of that well-dressed woman?
4   That your writing style is improving shows how hard you have worked.
5   The reason for choosing Simon as captain is that he has the most experience.
6   He refused to say what they were looking for.

Answers are in Appendix II.

2.4 PRONOUNS

Please read this passage:

> Richard Palmer and all the readers of *The Good Grammar Guide* are looking at pronouns. Pronouns stand in place of nouns; the job of nouns is done neatly and quickly by pronouns. When Richard Palmer and all the readers of the book have finished with looking at pronouns, Palmer and all readers will move on to adjectives. Adjectives are used to qualify nouns rather than replace nouns.

It contains just four sentences, but it's hard work, isn't it? It's clumsy, tedious and slow, and one shudders to think what it would be like to read *pages* of such a style.

When I composed that passage, I behaved as if there were no such things as **pronouns**. Here is how it reads in 'normal' English, with the eight pronouns highlighted:

> **We** are looking at pronouns, **which** stand in place of nouns, whose[10] job **they** do neatly and quickly. When **we**'ve done **that**, **we** shall move on to adjectives, **which** are used to qualify nouns rather than replace **them**.

10 You might think this is a pronoun, but it is a **relative adjective**, describing the noun job. This is explored in the next section.

It hardly needs saying that 2 is infinitely better than 1. Seven lines have been reduced to four, and four sentences to two: it reads comfortably and fluently. And it demonstrates how enormously useful pronouns are.

In essence, the pronoun is a straightforward device. The term combines the word for naming a thing or person (**noun**) with the Latin preposition *pro*, which means 'on behalf of' or 'standing in place of'. There are six types of pronoun:

1   **Personal**
2   **Demonstrative**
3   **Relative**
4   **Interrogative**
5   **Pronouns of number or quantity**
6   **The indefinite use of 'it'**

One important general point before we look at these in turn:

> **Every pronoun must have a definite *antecedent* – that is, it must be unambiguously clear which noun the pronoun refers back to.**

Failure to ensure this can lead to sentences like:

> Susan and her mother went shopping: she bought an expensive jewel case.

The reader has no idea which of the two women is denoted by **she**. Other examples of careless ambiguity are provided as we go: I hope there are no **un**intentional ones!

Personal pronouns

Personal pronouns stand for people – **I**, **we**, **you**, **they** and so on – and we use them a great deal. Their only complexity is that they are **inflected**: that is, they take, according to how they are used, one of four different forms:

nominative   accusative   possessive   reflexive

In the case of the pronoun **I**, these work out as follows:

nominative: I
accusative: me

possessive: mine
reflexive: myself

One could construct a perfectly accurate sentence where all four were employed:

> I want the money owed **me**: it is **mine**, and the rightful property of only **myself**.

This is rather clumsy, yes, and also somewhat repetitive or insistent! But all four pronouns are used correctly and show the four forms available.

The complete list runs:

nominative	accusative	possessive	reflexive
I	me	mine	myself
you (sing.)	you	yours	yourself
he	him	his	himself
she	her	hers	herself
we	us	ours	ourselves
you (pl.)	you	yours	yourselves
they	them	theirs	themselves

People make mistakes over personal pronouns, mainly because to choose between those four forms is sometimes tricky. Here are five sentences which use pronouns: they each contain at least one mistake. Can you spot them all? Answers on p. 189.

Exercise 8
1   Between you and I, I think he's going crazy.
2   She and me are going to the cinema.
3   Pass me them socks: they need a wash, pronto.
4   They think her is the only one what can do the job.
5   The rich don't care about we poor people.

Demonstrative pronouns

The term **demonstrative pronoun** may seem long and intimidating, but as I observed in Chapter One, it becomes comfortable enough if you associate it with the verb *to demonstrate*. For these pronouns point to things – they put a demonstrating focus on a particular object or concept:

> I like **this** very much: it's a lot better than **that**, and it's far superior to **those**.

Demonstrative pronouns need to be used with care, however. Always be sure you obey the antecedent rule defined above, and guard against vagueness, which the following sentence fails to do:

> He left her without saying a word, although he smiled shyly. **That** made her angry.

This isn't a bad effort in most respects – it's intriguing and quite dramatic. But it is not clear what **that** refers back to. Is it the fact that he left, that he left without saying a word, that he smiled shyly, or a combination of all three? We need to know, and we can't tell as it stands.

Relative pronouns

Relative pronouns **relate back** to a noun just used:

1   The book which I am reading is full of mistakes.
2   The woman who values her sanity will take no notice of soap powder advertisements.
3   The man whom I ran over in my car has made a miraculous recovery.

Again, always be sure you've made it clear to which noun you wish to refer back; in addition, always respect

(a) Any necessary **inflection** – as in **whom** (accusative) in 3.
(b) The **human** status (or otherwise) of your antecedent:

> **who** should only be used of humans, or occasionally such loved creatures as pets.
> **which** is used for everything else – all objects and all other beings.

And

(c) Take great care when punctuating. Here is 2 again, re-punctuated:

4   The woman, who values her sanity, will take no notice of soap
     powder advertisements.

Those commas make a big difference: 2 means that **any** woman who
values her sanity will ignore soap powder advertisements. It is a
recommendation to all women. Four speaks of **one** woman who will
ignore those advertisements and who happens also to value her sanity. It
is an **observation** about a specific woman.

In 2 there is a direct and intimate connection between women
ignoring advertisements and preserving their sanity. There is no such
connection in 4, because the commas make the two points quite separate,
thereby also changing the focus from the generic to the particular.[11]

Interrogative pronouns

I would suggest that this term is the easiest of the lot. An interrogative
pronoun is simply one that introduces a question:

1   **What** is that appalling noise?
2   **Who** is that idiot on the balcony?
3   **Whom** do you wish to see?
4   **Which** would you prefer – keeping quiet or having your face
     rearranged?

Notice that with interrogative pronouns, you do not for once have to
worry about **antecedents**. That is because a question naturally embodies
some suspense: it needs an answer. It is quite in order for the reader to be
kept waiting to find out what the pronoun refers to, since the questioner
is similarly awaiting information. However, **inflections** must still be
obeyed, as in 3.

---

11 This topic is further explored in Chapter Five; in addition, Chapter Seven has a sec-
    tion on the use of 'Which and That'.

Pronouns of number or quantity

These do the standard pronoun job of replacing a noun while also offering information as to amount or extent. They are quite straightforward, but care needs to be taken over **agreement**, since some such pronouns are singular, others plural:

1   Beware of buying second-hand clothes: **all** may be cheap, but **many** are of poor quality.
2   There is not **much** to be said.
3   Sorry, there is a big demand for tickets: we've only a **few** left, and you can have just **two** each.

The third sentence might puzzle you a little, in that **few** and **two** are normally thought of as adjectives, not pronouns. But both refer back to tickets and in effect take the place of the unnecessarily longer phrases **a few tickets** and **two tickets**. Thus in this instance they are pronouns.

The indefinite use of 'it'

We have encountered this already in Chapter One. In the main it is a trouble-free matter, not least because when used in such expressions as

it is raining   **it is midnight**   **How far is it to Babylon?**

it requires no antecedent. However, do not confuse this **indefinite** use with those occasions when it refers, or should refer, to something specific:

It bothered him   They were attached to **it**

In these instances, unless each it refers back clearly to an established creature or thing, the reader will be confused and possibly annoyed.

As signposted along the way, further material on pronouns can be found in Chapter Five.

2.5 ADJECTIVES

Adjectives qualify (give more information about) nouns. There are six types:

1   Descriptive   2   Possessive

3	Demonstrative	4	Relative
5	Interrogative	6	Of number or quantity

Descriptive adjectives

All the following highlighted words are descriptive adjectives:

a **scruffy** man	a **brilliant** intellect	**red** cabbage
rose-coloured glasses	the **wooden** horse	the **damp** cloth

Actually, the term descriptive adjective is pretty fatuous, not to say tautologous.[12] **All** adjectives have a descriptive function: **basic** or **ordinary** would be a more helpful term, since the other five types do a special, prescribed job. No matter: such adjectives should present no problems either of recognition or use.

Adjectives of this type can also be constructed from verbs:

1	The **astonished** policeman	2	The **borrowed** book
3	The **dancing** bear	4	The **leading** athlete

One and 2 use past particples, 3 and 4 present participles. In other circumstances, each one could be used as verb or part of a verb:

1a The riot **astonished** the policeman.
2a He **has borrowed** the book from me.
3a She **was dancing** for hours.
4a He **is leading** the field.

Many words have a multiple potential function, but they can only be one Part of Speech at a time. In the original examples, **astonished, borrowed, dancing** and **leading** are all adjectives, since they both qualify the relevant nouns and grammmatically depend on them.

Possessive adjectives

These closely resemble the **personal pronouns** studied a few pages ago – a fact that makes them both easy and difficult! The complete list of possessive adjectives is:

my   your (sing.)   his   her   its   our   your (pl.)   their

12 See Note 2 above.

His takes the same form as adjective and pronoun, and its function can only be determined by context:

1   Are those **his**?
2   Yes, those are **his** clothes.

In 1 **his** stands on its own, and is thus a pronoun. In 2 **his** is dependent upon the noun **clothes**, and is thus an adjective.

In all the other instances, the possessive adjective is distinct from the pronoun despite any superficial similarity:

Adjective	*Pronoun*
This is **my** money.	It's **mine**, okay?
Is this **your** book?	No, it's **yours**.
I'm **her** husband.	I'm **hers**.
That's **our** house	It belongs to **us**.
They were obliged to share **their** profit.	However, the expense had been all **theirs**.

Demonstrative adjectives

These are the same as **demonstrative pronouns**, except that they accompany a noun rather than stand on their own:

Give me **that** gun   Hand over **those** bullets   Sit in **this** chair

Like their pronoun cousins, **demonstrative** adjectives point to a noun, as if spotlighting it.

Relative adjectives

These work very like relative pronouns, but they accompany a noun:

He's a man **whose** behaviour is notorious.
I'll return at six, by **which** time the work must be finished.

For the most part relative adjectives are unproblematic. But watch out for two things, one elementary, the other subtle.

(a)   Do not, as many people do, confuse **whose** with **who's**. The latter is short for **who is** (pronoun + verb) and cannot be used adjectivally.

(b) As with relative pronouns, punctuate with great care. An incautious pair of commas can transform meaning:
   1   The man, whose work is successful, takes a break from time to time.
   2   The man whose work is successful takes a break from time to time.

Sentence 1 tells us of a particular adult male who works well and takes the occasional holiday. The two things are not directly linked even if some connection may be inferred. Two is intended as a **maxim**: it argues that all men who want to succeed in their work **must** take occasional holidays. Both sentences are perfectly satisfactory, of course, but you need to be clear about which meaning you want and whether that's the one you've chosen. Keep this subtle matter in mind at all times.

Interrogative adjectives

The easiest type of all, I would say. With their accompanying nouns, **interrogative** adjectives introduce questions:

   What time is it?
   Whose coffin is that?
   Which suit would you like to wear?

Adjectives of number or quantity

Number refers to **how many**, used with plural nouns; **quantity** refers to **how much**, used with singular nouns.

   Few people get to read their own obituaries.
   Twenty minutes remained when Clench scored the winner.
   Much heartache was caused by the Council's decision.
   Half her time was spent clearing up after others.

Be careful not to confuse, as many people do, **much** and **many**, and **less** and **fewer**:

   Much and **less** should only be used with **singular** nouns.
   Many and **fewer** should only be used with **plural** nouns.

Thus:

1   There was **less** trouble this time because **fewer** hooligans were
     present.
2   We haven't **much** time left – so **many** weeks have been wasted.

If in doubt about this, a moment's thought about the noun's status – is it
singular or plural? – should ensure that you get it right.

The three forms of adjectives

In addition to being divisible into six **types**, adjectives also have three
forms:

simple	comparative	superlative

There are two **regular** ways of forming the comparative and the
superlative. The first is to preface the adjective with the adverb **more** for
the former and the adverb **most** for the latter:

simple	comparative	superlative
difficult	more difficult	most difficult
ridiculous	more ridiculous	most ridiculous
terrible	more terrible	most terrible

You'll notice that each root adjective chosen is quite a long word, and
in fact all adjectives of three or more syllables take this form in the
comparative and superlative. So do all participles, even if they are of only
one syllable:

confusing	more confusing	most confusing
thrilling	more thrilling	most thrilling
bored	more bored	most bored
torn	more torn	most torn

Almost all other adjectives of one syllable take a different form in the
comparative and superlative, adding the suffix **-er** or **-est** instead of using
the adverbs:

thick	thicker	thickest
fast	faster	fastest
bright	brighter	brightest

Many **two**-syllable adjectives use the suffixes too –

easy	easier	easiest
tricky	trickier	trickiest
severe	severer	severest

– but not all:

absurd	more absurd	most absurd
dreadful	more dreadful	most dreadful
compact	more compact	most compact

Why some two-syllable-adjectives follow the suffix pattern while others add the adverb is hard to explain, and certainly not something one can codify in the form of a rule. The most helpful guide is *euphony*. To my ears **absurder, dreadfuller** and **compactest** sound clumsy and odd, something not true of **easier, trickier** or **severest**. However, you might think **severer** is rather awkward, as is its close counterpart **cleverer**, and prefer **more severe** and **more clever**. Those last two alternatives are perfectly correct, and often such choices are more a matter of taste and style than of formal accuracy.

In addition there are four **irregular** forms.

good	better	best
bad	worse	worst
far	farther/further	farthest/furthest
old	elder	eldest

Old is only semi-irregular, because of course the forms **older** and **oldest** are entirely correct.

Beware: there are certain adjectives whose meaning is **already absolute** and which therefore cannot assume comparative or superlative forms. Obvious examples would include:

dead   unique   eternal   circular   absolute

Nor can any number used as an adjective take the comparative or superlative form: it would be absurd to talk of

eight**er** hours   twent**iest** minutes   **most** thousand years

Finally, remember that the comparative can only operate when **two** things are being compared, and that **three or more** must be involved for the superlative to be used.

1 He was the **best** in the class. Correct
2 He was the **tallest** of the pair. Inorrect
3 She was the **fairer** of the two. Correct

Now try the exercise below, which tests grasp of pronouns and adjectives.

Exercise 9

A In this passage, can you identify three **relative**, four **demonstrative** and three **interrogative** pronouns?

'What's that?'
'What?'
'The book which you're reading.'
'Oh, that. It's a thriller by Gabriel Spiggott.'
'Who?'
'A guy whom I knew at school.'
'Those were the days, eh?'
'You must be joking. Anyone who thinks that must be potty.'

B Explain the difference between these sentences.

1 Students who plan their work sensibly tend to be more successful than others.
2 Students, who plan their work sensibly, tend to be more successful than others.

C Choose the correct alternative from the words given in brackets in these sentences.

1 Mozart wrote an astounding number of compositions: (all, each) are good, and (much, most) are sublime.
2 There are (less, fewer) people here than I expected.
3 We haven't (much, many) funds left: so (much, many) has been wasted.

---

continued

---

4   Not one of us (is, are) prepared to put up with this.

D   These sentences contain one mistake each. What are they?

1   Do you know who's briefcase this is?
2   Mind where your going.
3   Spurs and Arsenal met in the semi-final: they won 3–1.
4   Salvador Dali was quite unique.
5   I'll have the smallest half, please.

Answers are in Appendix II.

2.6 ADVERBS

Adverbs do an analogous job to adjectives: they give more information about other words. Whereas adjectives qualify nouns, adverbs modify verbs, adjectives or other adverbs.

A	He drove **stupidly**	She screamed **loudly**
B	**Remarkably** careless	**Highly** intelligent
C	**Very** well	**Quite** quickly

In A the two adverbs modify the verbs **drove** and **screamed**, in B the adjectives **careless** and **intelligent**, and in C the adverbs **well** and **quickly**.
    There are seven types of one-word adverb.[13]

1	**Manner**	2	**Place**	3	**Time**
4	**Degree, quantity or extent**				
5	**Number**	6	**Relative**	7	**Interrogative**

Adverbs of manner

These give us information about how the verb is performed:

---

13   There are several further types of adverb *phrase* and adverb *clause*; for a full treatment of these, see Chapter five.

1   He ate his food **rapidly**.
2   **Gingerly** she stepped into the pool.
3   They greeted the news **joyously**.
4   He read the document **conscientiously** but **slowly**.

All those examples end in **-ly**, as indeed do the majority of adverbs of manner. Quite a few take a different form, however: **fast** and **well** are two obvious examples.

Adverbs of place

These tell us **where** the verb is performed.

1   He visited Amsterdam and had a wonderful time **there**.
2   Come **hither**.
3   You cannot smoke **here**; the smoking area is **nearby**.

Adverbs of time

These tell us **when** the verb is performed.

1   It poured with rain **yesterday**.
2   I **often** eat sweets and I want one **now**.
3   The train arrived **late**.

Adverbs of degree, quantity or extent

These all have to do with **amount** or **proportion**, answering the implicit question 'how much?':

1   You've **nearly** finished it.
2   He's said **enough**.
3   They were **very** annoyed.

Adverbs of number

These are separate from adverbs of time and degree, referring to an exact number :

1   The postman always rings **twice**.
2   He increased his savings **fourfold**.

3   Robert tried heroin – **once**.

Notice that 3 could, by being repunctuated or rearranged, take on different meanings. As it stands, the sentence stresses that Robert tried heroin **on a single occasion**. This next version –

3a   Robert tried heroin once.

– means that he did so **in the past** (as in 'once upon a time'), and that many individual occasions may have been involved. And in this version –

3b   Once Robert tried heroin . . .

– **once** has the force of 'From the moment that', and we need a further clause to complete the sense, as in:

3c   **Once** Robert tried heroin, his whole life collapsed.

Relative adverbs

These connect two clauses, like relative pronouns and relative adjectives:

1   He found out **where** the party was.
2   November is a time **when** everyone feels lethargic.
3   Tell me **why** you're upset.

Interrogative adverbs

Like their pronoun and adjective cousins, these are entirely straightforward, introducing direct questions:

1   **Where** is my drink?
2   **When** are you going to do some work?
3   **Why** are we waiting?

The three forms of adverbs

Just like adjectives, adverbs have three possible forms:

simple   comparative   superlative

The majority of adverbs – including all those ending in **-ly** – follow this pattern for the two modified forms:

quickly	more quickly	most quickly
rarely	more rarely	most rarely
often	more often	most often

As with adjectives, however, one-syllable adverbs use suffixed forms:

soon	sooner	soonest
fast	faster	fastest
hard	harder	hardest

There are also two **irregular** adverbs:

well	better	best
badly	worse	worst

Forming the comparative and the superlative is generally easier with adverbs than it is with adjectives, and if you understand how the latter work, you should have no trouble with single-word adverbs. But please read the brief section that follows before we move on to **prepositions**.

Interim summary

It may occur to you that compared to the other Parts of Speech covered so far, I have breezed through this study of adverbs. That is because I have only looked at **simple**, one-word adverbs. **Adverbials** – words or groups of words that have an adverbial function – are the most frequently-used structures in English, and many of them are highly complex. You stand a much better chance of using them well if you first master the basic functions that adverbs perform. The elementary approach adopted here should provide a sound platform on which to build a full understanding of the advanced material in Chapter Five.

2.7 PREPOSITIONS

As its formation suggests, **preposition** means 'placed before'. Prepositions are words placed before a noun or pronoun to show relationship between persons or things or actions.

1   They live **in** the country.
2   She sat **beside** me.
3   Tell me **about** yourself.
4   Keep **off** the grass.

There are some fifty English prepositions. A full list would not serve any useful purpose; what is important is that you take note of these two points, the first of which cropped up in Exercise 1 above:

All prepositions take the accusative case.

In English the accusative case is 'invisible' most of the time; as we've discovered, however, such inflection comes into play with several pronouns, and the accusative form must always be used:

5   He sent a letter **to me**.
6   We don't know anything **about her**.
7   They could see the roaring torrent **beneath them**.
8   The house **opposite us** is being renovated.

Many prepositions can double as adverbs.

By definition a preposition must operate with a noun or pronoun. If the latter is omitted, the preposition changes function, becoming an adverb:

9   He stood **outside** the building.   **preposition**
10   She went **outside**.   **adverb**
11   **Above** us the waves.   **preposition**
12   See **above**.   **adverb**

Prepositions help form **phrases**; these can be adjectival, adverbial or noun phrases, structures further studied in Chapter Five.

2.8 CONJUNCTIONS

Junction means 'joining'; **con** is Latin for 'with'. Conjunctions are words which join a word, phrase or clause with another word, phrase or clause.

1   Whisky **and** water   (**word to word**)
2   Shaken **but** not stirred   (**word to phrase**)
3   Do you want the cassette tape **or** the
    compact disc?   (**phrase to phrase**)

4   Do it, **and** as soon as possible.   (**clause to phrase**)
5   I can't go to the concert **because** I'm broke.   (**clause to clause**)

Strictly speaking, conjunctions are divided into two types – **coordinating conjunctions** and **subordinating conjunctions**. The distinction is interesting, and is looked at further in Chapter Four; from an ordinary writer's point of view, however, the key thing with conjunctions is not to overdo them! Even sophisticated writers can easily fall into the trap of cluttering up their sentences with too many **and**s, **but**s, **or**s and **because**s. The deft use of punctuation – particularly colons and semi-colons – will often preclude the need for a conjunction, and you should try to use every joining device in the course of your work to prevent boredom, both on your part and the reader's.

2.9 INTERJECTIONS

Well, I reckon this sentence takes care of the whole topic!
    Interjections are 'verbal tics'. Some of them should be avoided at all costs anyway, and must certainly never contaminate formal writing:

er/um   you know   I mean   sort of

Other interjections are however perfectly permissible, although they should be used sparingly and isolated via punctuation:

oh   well   oh well   okay   yes   no

1   **Oh,** you've changed!
2   **Oh well,** if you won't do it, there's no more to be said.
3   **Okay,** so I'm lazy.
4   **Yes,** you're intelligent; **no,** you're not studious.

In each instance, the highlighted interjection has no grammatical connection with the rest of the sentence. It is a mild exclamation or introductory message whose omission would not alter the sense of what is said. But interjections do add tonal colour – nowhere better demonstrated than in oaths:

Goddammit!   Strewth!   Crikey!   Blast!

Those examples are remarkably restrained on my part, but I hope you get the general idea.

Chapter 3

Inflections

3.1 PRELIMINARY

An inflection means a change in the form of a word according to the job it is doing. English is not highly inflected, especially compared to several European languages, but there are still many times when inflection is required. This section looks at all of them, although it is not an exhaustive treatment. Occasionally my remarks will be brief, as we have come across some of these instances of inflection during the first two chapters.

3.2 IRREGULAR VERBS

A regular verb is one whose forms are determined by rules and is thus predictable. If we take the three verbs **look**, **listen** and **perform** we find they all behave alike when changes are required:

1 They add -s to form the third person present singular.
2 The past participle and simple past tense are formed by adding -ed.
3 The present participle is formed by adding -ing.

There are well over 300 verbs which do not obey one or more of these procedures. Space precludes listing them all; besides, I think that would be tedious rather than helpful – both to read and to write. What is worthwhile is to look at the various kinds of irregular verb, with examples of each.

The eight classes of irregular verb

A A number of verbs seem to be entirely regular, but they incorporate a change of spelling in one or more of their forms. For example:

(a) **stop** takes a double **p** in both participle forms and in the simple past:

stopping   **stopped**   **they stopped**

(b) So does hop:

hopping   **hopped**   **she hopped**

It is especially important to get (b) right, because you otherwise confuse it with hope, whose same forms are:

hoping   **hoped**   **we hoped**

(c) **panic** adds a **k** to all three forms; the hard **c** of the original would otherwise be softened by the **i** and **e**:

panicking   **panicked**   **you panicked**

(d) **die** is regular in past participle and simple past forms, but changes spelling in the present participle:

dying[1]

Such verbs are, arguably, **minorly inconsistent** rather than **irregular**. Pedantically, that may be so; but they cause writers a lot of trouble, and in my view thus earn their place here.

B Verbs whose only irregularity is the ending used for the past participle and simple past. For example:

have: had   **learn: learnt**   **burn: burnt**   **send: sent**

---

1 If you use the verb **dye** in present participle form, the e must be retained to avoid confusion: **dyeing**.

C Verbs whose simple past is regular but whose past participle takes a different form:

He **mowed** the lawn	They were **mown** down
The crowd **swelled**	Her face **was swollen**

D Verbs whose ending for the simple past and past participle is the same but irregular. In addition, there is a change of vowel or vowel-number:

teach: taught   seek: sought   sell: sold   keep: kept

E Verbs whose past participle ends in **-n** and which also have an irregular simple past form. The base vowel is affected as well:

infinitive	past participle	simple past
break	broken	He broke cover
take	taken	We took stock
blow	blown	She blew her top
see	seen	I saw a ghost
run	run	I ran a mile

F Verbs whose forms do not change at all:

infinitive	past participle	simple past
cut	cut	He cut his finger
let	let	She let them in
cast	cast	He cast off the ship
broadcast	broadcast	She broadcast the news

All verbs are inflected in the third person singular, adding **-s**, and these Category F irregulars are no exception, which prevents confusion between present and past: **she lets them in/ she let them in**. In the other five persons, however, present and past forms are the same:

present	simple past
I cut my finger	I cut my finger
You let him get away	You let him get away
We cast caution aside	We cast caution aside
They broadcast daily	They broadcast daily

Context will normally establish whether the writer intends the present or the past; if you find, when writing yourself, that the context doesn't

resolve ambiguity, select a different form of the tense you require that is
fully clear.

G Verbs which have no discernible ending and whose past participle
and simple past forms are the same. A base-vowel change also occurs.

infinitive	past participle	simple past
sit	sat	They sat down
stand	stood	He stood up
lead	led	She led him astray

H The most irregular type of all. These verbs have no discernible ending;
the past participle and simple past forms differ; the vowels change.

infinitive	past participle	simple past
come	come	It came to me
go	gone	They went away
begin	begun	She began to read
lie	lain	He lay down

That last one is important, because **lie** seems to cause a lot of problems.
For a start, it has two different meanings, and they follow quite separate
grammatical forms. The above example uses **lie** in the sense of 'to be
prone'; if the meaning of 'to tell an untruth' is required, the verb becomes
regular:

lie   lied   He lied to me

The matter is further complicated by the fact that **lay** is not only the past
tense of **lie** but a verb in its own right. It is **transitive** (**lie** is intransitive)
and has several meanings:

1	To deposit	**He lays his life on the line.**
2	To present	**Let me lay my cards on the table.**
3	To impose	**They're laying the blame on me.**
4	To produce	**Hens lay eggs.**
5	To arrange	**Lay the table, would you?**

That is not a comprehensive list: it omits amongst others a somewhat
raunchy meaning. However, if you ever refer to **laying around the house**,
don't be surprised if you incur a few giggles and/or odd looks! More

seriously, take great care not to confuse **lie** and **lay**: few things look or sound more illiterate. Incidentally, the past participle of **lay** is **laid**, as is its form in the simple past.

Irregular verbs can infuriate. There are so many types, and their formation often seems quite irrational. Fortunately, the vast majority of them are frequently used, so one quickly learns, if only through error. In addition, the inflections occurring in irregular verbs are the trickiest, most complicated there are: get a good working grasp of those and the others should be plain sailing.

3.3 CONTRACTED NEGATIVE VERBS

Quite a mouthful, that term! Happily, the usage it defines is a fairly simple matter.

In the previous chapter we looked at the sixteen **auxiliary verbs** (p. 35). All of them can be contracted in the negative form – something never possible with any main verb:

verb	standard negative	contracted negative
can	cannot	can't
do	do not/does not	don't/doesn't
ought	ought not	oughtn't
shall	shall not	shan't
will	will not	won't

And to prove that you can't do this with ordinary[2] main verbs:

discuss	not discuss	**discussn't**
eat	not eat	**eatn't**

The bold-type negatives are self-evidently absurd.

---

2   The three primary auxiliary verbs – **be**, **have** and **do** – can also operate as main verbs. **Be** and **have** can be contracted in either function; the need to contract **do** as a main verb never arises:

Auxiliary	Main
It isn't raining	He isn't rich
I haven't been there	We haven't time
She doesn't smoke	–

3.4 OTHER INFLECTIONS AFFECTING VERBS

Apart from contracted negatives and all the inflections that occur in irregular verbs, there are three other instances when the verb changes form:

1 The third-person indicative singular of all verbs adds -s or -es to the root.

he departs   she leaves   he discusses   it goes

2 Present participles are formed by adding -ing. Normally this is straightforward, but sometimes the spelling changes:

lie: lying   die: dying   come: coming   judge: judging

As the last two examples indicate, nearly all verbs ending in -e drop that letter when forming the present participle. There are exceptions, however – designed to prevent the confusion of similar words with separate meanings:

sing: singing   singe: singeing
die: dying   dye: dyeing
swing: swinging   swinge: swingeing[3]

3 Past participles are formed by adding -d or -ed. (See above, p. 52)
4 Both present and past participles are also used to form different **tenses**. (See above, p. 30)
5 Verbs can change form in their different **moods**. (See above, pp. 33–35)

3.5 NOUN PLURALS

Most nouns have a singular and a plural form. (We look at the exceptions shortly.) Normally the plural is formed by adding -s to the singular noun:

eggs   cows   televisions   waters   saxophones

---

3   The verb is archaic; the participle/adjective means 'huge'. The recently popular word **whingeing** follows the same principle.

Words whose singular already ends in -s, -sh or -ch add -es in the plural:

kisses   **masses**   **brushes**   **fishes**   **marches**

Irregularities

1 Common, collective and abstract nouns whose singular ends in -y preceded by a consonant drop the -y in the plural and add -ies instead:

family/families	party/parties	city/cities
aviary/aviaries	misery/miseries	pity/pities
(Cf. boy/boys	guy/guys	jay/jays)

1a Proper names ending in -y preceded by a consonant simply add -s in the plural:

Kennedys   **Marys**   **O'Reillys**

2 Seven nouns change their vowel in the plural form:

man/men	woman/women	foot/feet	tooth/teeth
goose/geese	mouse/mice	louse/lice	

3 Three nouns add -en to form their plural:

ox/oxen   child/children   brother/brethren[4]

4 A number of nouns change their final -f to -v and add -s:

wife/wives	knife/knives	leaf/leaves
half/halves	wolf/wolves	loaf/loaves

5 Foreign words
   English has borrowed tens of thousands of words from other languages. Sometimes they obey their original plural form (**crises**); sometimes they assume an English plural (**syllabuses**, not **syllabi**) and sometimes either is possible (**cactuses** or **cacti**).

---

4   In religious contexts only – e.g. The Plymouth Brethren. In ordinary contexts **brothers** should be used.

Naturally, a full list is out of the question. But take particular care with the following, which many people get wrong:

singular	plural
criterion	criteria
phenomenon	phenomena
curriculum	curricula
medium	media

6 Invariable nouns
Some nouns are used only in the singular:

music   homework   snow   stuff

They should always be used with a singular verb even if the implicit sense is plural:

1 Music in every form delights me.
2 Snow has fallen, snow on snow.

Other nouns are used only in the plural:

shears   thanks   people   trousers[5]

Similarly, they must be accompanied by a plural verb, even if the implicit sense is singular:

3 That's wonderful: thanks are in order.
4 My favourite trousers have been ruined.

And a few nouns have the same singular and plural form:

sheep   partridge   aircraft   innings

Such words should always be used in close conjunction with a word that clearly establishes **number**:

5 You will sometimes hear the noun **trouser** used by assistants in men's outfitters. I'm sorry, but I think it's ridiculous, managing to be both tacky and pretentious. However, it can be used sensibly as an adjective – **trouser suit, trouser-leg**.

5	Your sheep is missing.	5a	Your sheep have escaped.
6	The aircraft is damaged.	6a	They've grounded all aircraft.

3.6 THE GENITIVE OF NOUNS

We've come across the genitive in Chapter One in the subsections devoted to the apostrophe and case. I pointed out then that **all** apostrophes denote omission and that the notion of a possessive apostrophe is erroneous. In simple genitives like **John's book** and **the girls' clothes** the apostrophe denotes the omission of letters that were included in the original Anglo-Saxon structures: **Joh<u>nes</u> book** and **the girl<u>ses</u> clothes**. As the years went by, the extra syllable was elided: hence the apostrophe.

The genitive case, then, is formed in the singular by the addition of -'s and in most plurals by the addition of the apostrophe only.

the man's tie	**the woman's salary**	(singular)
the boys' playground	**the employees' canteen**	(plural)

Take care with irregular plurals (see the previous section):

men's handkerchiefs	**the media's influence**
the Kennedys' tragedy	**geese's migration**

Singular nouns ending in -s seem to be somewhat problematic, in that a lot of people make mistakes when forming the genitive. Strictly speaking, singular nouns of one or two syllables ending in -s should add an apostrophe and a further **s**:

The class's behaviour   **Jesus's life**

This principle has been much disparaged of late; many authorities find it needlessly meticulous, if not downright pedantic. I would defend it on the grounds of pronunciation: when we speak the above phrases we add the extra – **class's** and **Jesus's** – and I think it makes sense to signal that fact when writing them down. However, the point is a minor one and largely a matter of taste; certainly it is now accepted usage to employ the apostrophe only.

For all longer words ending in -s the addition of a further **s** looks and sounds awkward, so only the apostrophe is used:

the hippopotamus' grin   Coriolanus' mother[6]

Not all genitives denote possession as such. Study these:

St Mark's Gospel	the man's story	(origin)
a winter's night	a Ploughman's Lunch	(description)
in three hours' time	one day's respite	(measurement)

None of those six phrases denotes belonging in the strict sense. Indeed, the first is often expressed as **The Gospel** *according* **to St Mark**, which is distinct from any notion of ownership. And a Ploughman's Lunch does not signify a midday meal belonging to a tiller of the soil: it's a pretentious marketing phrase for 'bread and cheese'!

The genitive can also be used to express the role of **subject**:

the client's claim	(i.e. the client claimed)
the wrestler's submission	(i.e. the wrestler submitted)

6   **NB** Take great care over *placing* the apostrophe. I shudder to think of the number of times I've encountered this kind of thing:

  Dicken's books   Henry Jame's novels

Such apparently minor errors are not just comic: they suggest someone who is simply not thinking.

Or as object:

> the thief's pardon   (i.e. someone pardoned the thief)
> the discs' reissue   (i.e. someone reissued the discs)

The genitive's inflections remain the same whatever their function. Sometimes, however, it is better to use a different structure to express the genitive. In these examples –

> **His misery's worst part was the loneliness.**
> **The course's single most attractive feature was the year spent abroad.**

– the genitive structures are somewhat bloated and would be better expressed using **of**:

> **The worst part of his misery was the loneliness.**
> **The single most attractive feature of the course was the year spent abroad.**

In general the -'s genitive is used for personal and animate nouns and the **of**- genitive for inanimate and abstract nouns. But such things are finally matters of taste and style rather than 'rules': if, as always, you listen to what you write, you will invariably make the right choice.

3.7 PREFIXES AND SUFFIXES

These are morphemes[7] added to the front of words (prefix) or to the end (suffix) to form new meanings.

1   noble: **ig**noble
2   interested: **un**interested/**dis**interested[8]
3   face: **pre**face
4   late: **trans**late

---

7   **Morpheme:** the smallest divisible speech element having a meaning or grammatical function.
8   The two prefixed words are not synonyms! **Uninterested** means 'bored'; **disinterested** means 'impartial'. See Exercise 1 above, item 2.

5   happy: happi**ness**
6   rely: reli**able**
7   captain: captain**cy**
8   relation: relation**ship**

Strictly speaking, I suppose, the majority of prefixes and more than a
few suffixes are not inflectional devices, since they do not alter the
grammatical function or structure of the words to which they're added.
Of the eight examples above, only 4, 5 and 6 effect such a change of
function:

4   changes an **adjective** into a **verb**
5   changes an **adjective** into a **noun**
6   changes a **verb** into an **adjective**

But all prefixes and suffixes have to do with **morphology** (the study of
word structure) and all, as noted, alter meaning. Whether genuine
inflections or otherwise, they are a valuable resource for any writer, even
if several are easy to confuse. You will find a substantial guide to those in
Chapter Five.

3.8 ADDITIONAL INFLECTIONS

All **personal pronouns** are inflected, as are some forms of the relative,
demonstrative and interrogative pronouns. This has been covered in full
on pp. 47–8. **Adjectives** and **adverbs** are inflected in the comparative and
superlative forms. This too has been dealt with, on pp. 55–7 and 60–1.

Try the summarising exercise below; the next chapter looks at **syntax**.

Exercise 10
A In these sentences, put the verb in brackets into the form
designated on the right.

1   Two minutes into the interview she   **(past tense)**
    (panic).
2   His left knee was dreadfully (swell).   **(past participle)**
3   We are (begin) to get somewhere.   **(present participle)**

continued

4   He (lie) motionless on the bed.   **(past tense)**
5   They (lie) to the police throughout.   **(past tense)**

B As economically as you can, add something to these sentences to ensure that the past tense is signalled:

1   TV-AM broadcast daily.
2   We let them off with a caution.

C Change the highlighted nouns – and, if necessary, their accompanying verbs – from singular to plural:

1   I prefer **a kiss** to **a march**.
2   It almost seems as if **Kennedy** was doomed from the start.
3   The **party** did not please the **guy**.
4   What is your **criterion** when judging intelligence?

D These sentences all include one mistake. Can you put each one right?

1   Are you telling me you dislike all Mahler's musics?
2   Would you pass me that shears?
3   Paul Gascoigne was once Spur's most talented player.
4   Many people find the medias' intrusiveness objectionable.
5   I want to talk to you tonight about childrens' rights.

E Form the opposite meaning of these words by adding a prefix.
1 normal 2 opportune 3 spell 4 array 5 associate

F Add a suffix to change these words into the form designated:

1   uneasy   (adjective into abstract noun)
2   detest   (verb into abstract noun)
3   joy   (noun into adjective)
4   urgent   (adjective into adverb)
5   depend   (verb into adjective)

Answers are in Appendix II.

Chapter 4

Syntax

4.1 PRELIMINARY

The word **syntax** bothers a lot of people – including me, I might add! I find it slippery: it is difficult to pin down exactly what it means or can mean – an elusiveness confirmed when consulting *The Shorter Oxford English Dictionary*:

> **syntax:**
> (A) The arrangement of words (in their appropriate forms) by which their connection and relation in a sentence are shown . . . Also, the constructional uses . . . characteristic of an author.
> (B) The department of grammar which deals with the established usages of grammatical construction and the rules deduced therefrom.

There is a fundamental difference between the two definitions. The first limits **syntax** to matters of word-relationship and word-order – a significant issue, certainly, but much narrower than B, which almost makes **syntax** synonymous with **grammar** itself.

It is definition A that governs the material here. The two previous chapters have already dealt with much that definition B encompasses, and there is further such material in the next chapter. This one looks at how words operate in groups – in phrases, clauses and various types of sentence – and how you can best arrange them to ensure the meaning required.

4.2 PHRASES

So far in this book we have largely focused on individual words. To be sure, this has occasionally involved looking at compounds, as in tenses (**we have eaten**), comparative adjectives (**more difficult**) and the like; nevertheless, each topic has looked at an individual part of speech and the various forms it may take.

A **phrase** is a structure that may employ several parts of speech in the expression of a single idea:

1   on the table
2   All things considered
3   parts of speech
4   Behind every successful man

1   Uses a **preposition**, an **adjective** (the definite article[1] **the**) and a **noun**.
2   Uses an **adjective**, a **noun** and another **adjective** formed from a **past participle**.
3   Uses a **plural noun**, a **preposition** and a **singular noun**.
4   Uses a **preposition**, two successive **adjectives** and a **noun**.

Phrases are thus plural constructions and quite complex compared to individual words. However, although all the above make **some** sense, none of them makes **complete** sense. A phrase is never an **independent** structure: to acquire complete sense it needs to become part of a larger formation that identifies **subject, action** and **time**.

1a   He threw up on the table.
2a   All things considered, the tour was a disaster.
3a   I've had enough of parts of speech for the time being.
4a   Behind every successful man there's a good woman – or an understanding bank-manager.

Each original phrase has been placed in a context which makes complete sense. The subjects and verbs define and illuminate the phrases – and vice versa. Four intriguing **sentences** result.

---

1   This term and its 'brother' the **indefinite article** (**a, an**) are fully explained in Chapter Five.

Before we proceed further, try this little exercise.

Exercise 11

Which of the following six are sentences, and which are phrases?
Answers below.

1 Cabinets full of records.
2 It is raining.
3 Given your considerable abilities.
4 This year I'm not going to be lucky.
5 Underneath the resplendent sweep of the bridge.
6 The dilapidated old shed with the chicken-coop next to it.

Only 2 and 4 are sentences: all the others require a verb if they are to make complete sense. The exercise, simple enough, visually stresses an important point: **sentences** can be very short, and mere **phrases** can be quite long. The shortest structure in those six is the three-word 2, but it's a complete **sentence**; 6 already has eleven words but will need even more to become independent. That neatly sets up our next topic.

4.3 THE SIMPLE SENTENCE

This term means a sentence that has just one **finite verb**. That is the **only** criterion: in this usage **simple** has nothing to do with length or easiness.

1 It **is raining**.
2 The council **condemned** the dilapidated old shed with the chicken-coop next to it.
3 The highlight of the evening, and in my view one of the greatest performances ever heard in this country, **was** his scintillating rendition of Liszt's B Minor Sonata.

Sentence 1 could hardly be shorter or easier; 2 is quite substantial; 3 is long and involved. But each one is a **simple sentence**, as the highlighted single finite verb confirms.

4.4 DOUBLE AND MULTIPLE SENTENCES

These next examples consist entirely of **simple sentences**.

1   It is raining. I am fed up.
2   The doorbell rang. He rose eagerly to his feet. The dog started barking ferociously.

If you were to write like that for any length of time, the resultant jerkiness would soon irritate. That danger is easily averted:

1a   It is raining **and** I am fed up.
2a   The doorbell rang **and** he rose eagerly to his feet, **but** the dog started barking ferociously.

1a is a **double sentence**: simple sentence + simple sentence.
2a is a **multiple sentence**: simple sentence + simple sentence + simple sentence.

Theoretically, there is no limit to the number of simple sentences you can include in a multiple sentence. However, frequent and lengthy multiple sentences are just as irksome to read as a string of simple sentences, if not more so:

2b   The doorbell rang and he rose eagerly to his feet, but the dog started barking ferociously and he gave it a biscuit and shut it in the kitchen to prevent trouble, so then he was able to admit his visitor.

Reading that sentence is hard, unrewarding work: even replacing some of the conjunctions with appropriate punctuation wouldn't make it much better. The writer crams too much into the sentence, rendering it breathless and blurred. In addition, greater structural variety is required, which is where the use of **clauses** comes in.

All sentences within a double or multiple sentence have equal **status**. In all the examples looked at so far, each sentence could stand on its own, making complete sense: that is indeed the definition of a sentence. Another way of putting it is that a simple sentence consists of a **main clause**, a double sentence of **two main clauses**, and a multiple sentence of **three or more main clauses**. However, clauses can also be **subordinate**, helping to form **complex sentences**, which is our next topic.

4.5 CLAUSES AND COMPLEX SENTENCES

We looked briefly at these in Chapter One. What I did not go into during that preliminary study was **the difference between a clause and a sentence**, which is not easy either to understand or define. Indeed, unless you already *know* the difference, I would guess that these definitions offered by *The Shorter Oxford Dictionary* will not only fail to illuminate but actually increase your confusion. First, 'sentence':

> **A series of words in connected speech or writing, forming the grammatically complete expression of a single thought.**

And now 'clause':

> **A short sentence; a distinct member of a sentence, one containing a subject and a predicate.**

The most one can deduce from all that seems to be:

> **All sentences are clauses, or contain several clauses; but a single clause does not necessarily form a sentence.**

And a fat lot of help that is, no doubt prompting the reaction, 'Thanks a whole bunch!' I hope I can clear things up by studying some examples, in the form of a little exercise.

Exercise 12

Which of these is a sentence, which a clause?

1   Although you broke the window.
2   I forgive you.
3   I have a hunch that.
4   You dislike cheese.

All four start with capitals and end with full stops; all four have a subject and a finite verb – as follows:

	Subject	Finite verb
1	you	broke

2	I	forgive
3	I	have
4	You	dislike

But do all four express 'a complete thought'?

I trust you can see that 1 and 3 do not: we need more information for them to satisfy fully. Both are left hanging in the air. In 1 the use of 'although' sets up an expectation that is not fulfilled, while 3 is even more frustrating, leaving us ignorant of what this 'hunch' is about.

Two and four are complete. They may be somewhat bald, even uninteresting; nevertheless, they require nothing else to make complete grammatical and intellectual sense.

However, it is relatively easy to make 1 and 3 part of an authentic sentence: we can merge them with 2 and 4.

5   Although you broke the window, I forgive you.
6   I have a hunch that you dislike cheese.

These make complete sense, and are now, perhaps, more interesting!

Five and six now consist of two clauses – each has two subjects and two finite verbs. And both consist of a **main clause** and a **subordinate clause**. The latter term describes a clause that cannot stand on its own –

Although you broke the window . . .
I have a hunch that . . .

Subordinate clauses are grammatical juniors, dependent on the main clause for complete sense. They are not subordinate in any other way; they need not be stylistically inferior, and indeed may be more informative than the main clause they depend on, as in this example:

7   If you go on with a diet that consists exclusively of cottage cheese, dry toast and Brazil nuts, I shall worry.

The main clause is **I shall worry**: it is rather feeble in view of what precedes it, a sad anticlimax to what was promising to be a fairly arresting sentence. But although that previous clause is much more interesting in every other way, it remains grammatically subordinate: it could not stand on its own.

So to summarise:

All sentences have a subject and finite verb and make complete and independent sense.

All clauses have a subject and finite verb too, but they do not *necessarily* **make complete and independent sense.**

In case you're still not fully clear or happy, some further examples may help:

1 The man was frightened.
2 The man was frightened: the dog looked vicious.
3 The man was frightened, because the dog looked vicious.

Sentence 1 is a **simple sentence** consisting of one **main clause**.

Sentence 2 is a **double sentence** consisting of two **simple sentences/ main clauses**. The colon signals a connection between them, but they are grammatically independent.

Sentence 3 is a **complex sentence**: it has a **main clause** and a **subordinate clause**. Let's analyse it briefly.

Although the **sense** of 3 is virtually identical to that of 2, the sentence works in a grammatically different way. The first clause can stand on its own, of course, as in 1; but if the second clause is isolated it fails to make complete sense:

3a Because the dog looked vicious . . .

I put in those dots (**ellipsis**) to show how the clause 'hangs in the air'. **Because** is a **subordinating conjunction**: here it signals a link between the dog's vicious appearance and . . . well, what? As 3a stands, it could be anything: it must be specified for the structure to make full sense – i.e. for it to become a **sentence**. Intriguingly, we can achieve that by **adding** the clause that originally started the sentence:

3b Because the dog looked vicious, the man was frightened.

As always, forget those bogus purists who say one should never begin a sentence with a conjunction: the only real criterion here is which is more effective – the word-order in 3 or 3b? What is **your** view? Think about it for a moment, and see if you agree with my remarks that follow.

There isn't much in it, but I prefer 3, which is punchier than 3b. The dog's vicious appearance is the most dramatic thing in the sentence, and has greater impact, I'd say, if left till the end. In 3b, the main clause is rather anticlimactic, almost as if we could have guessed it after such an opening. But my argument is a subtle matter of taste and style: if you prefer 3b, fine – it's a clear and accurate sentence.

Sometimes, though, the positioning of clauses makes a decisive difference to meaning or tone or both. Study these two sentences carefully:

4   The record **which John wanted** was out of stock.
4a   The record was out of stock, **which John wanted**.

Sentence 4 means that a particular record that John wanted was unavailable.

Sentence 4a is tricky. **Either** it's a rather incompetent attempt to say the same thing as 4 **or** it's a deft way of saying something else entirely – **that John wanted the record to be unavailable.** Maybe his kid-brother/ sister/wife/father was planning to pollute the home's aural atmosphere with something he found excruciating, and was thus delighted that the purchase couldn't be made!

The record was out of stock, which John wanted.

Similarly, how do these sentences differ?

5   Although I understand you've not been well, this work is inadequate.
5a   This work is inadequate, although I understand you've not been well.

If you were the student concerned, which one would you prefer to hear? They *seem* to say exactly the same thing . . . but 5a is surely far more sympathetic. The speaker suggests that the student's recent illness explains and indeed mitigates a poor performance. Five regards the recent illness as an irrelevance: the speaker wants the student to realise that such work won't do and that no excuses are admissible.

The differences in word-order here primarily affect **tone**, but you can see that tonal qualities can in turn affect **meaning**. Certainly, Listener 5 would go away from the interview in a very different frame of mind from Listener 5a.

4.6 INTERIM SUMMARY

I've called this 'An Interim Summary' because there is a lot of additional material on clauses in the next chapter. But it is my hope that you have already realised that **complex sentences** – i.e. those that consist of a main clause + one or more subordinate clauses – are the writer's most valuable friend.

The most important aspect of all writing is that it should always be **clear**, and I am certainly not urging you to write complex sentences for the sake of it. Whatever your task and whatever its length, you will regularly need to spell things out in as direct a fashion as possible; on those occasions the simple sentence and its elder brothers, the double and multiple sentence, will probably be your best choice. But they have their limitations. As we've seen, in even a six-clause multiple sentence, each clause has the same status. Gradations of tone and meaning are very hard to effect in such sentences: this is indeed as it should be, because they aim at directness, not subtlety.

But on many other occasions the success of your writing will depend on **nuance** – i.e. subtle shades of tone and meaning, the kind of precision that simple, double and multiple sentences ultimately cannot achieve on their own. That is why **syntax** is a fundamental and genuinely creative matter. In the simple sentence family, word-order is not significant, provided basic rules of logic and grammatical sense are obeyed. Complex sentences allow you to build meaning and effect in a fashion both aesthetically pleasing and pithily exact, and they do so because their placing of words is hardly less important than the choice of the words themselves.

Finally, a brief look at how the placing of individual words, rather than phrases or clauses, can alter meaning.

4.7 THE RIGHT WORD IN THE RIGHT PLACE

During the study of adverbs of number in Chapter Two, we saw how the word **once** could have a different function or meaning according to where it was placed. In the same way, see how the exact location of **only** in these three sentences effects three separate meanings:

1 Mark **only** wanted to see Ginny.
2 Mark wanted **only** to see Ginny.
3 Mark wanted to see **only** Ginny.

Sentence 1 is fairly casual, or possibly defensive/apologetic. It means that Mark **merely** wanted to see Ginny.

Sentence 2 is extremely forceful. It means that Mark had just one thing in mind – **seeing Ginny**. Nothing else mattered.

Sentence 3 means that Mark wanted to see Ginny **alone**. Presumably someone else turned out to be present, and the implication is that Mark was fed up about this! Alternatively, it could mean that Mark wanted to see Ginny and **no one else**: maybe she wasn't there, or maybe he single-mindedly went in search of her. Both versions are also forceful, but with different meanings from 2.

A second, final example. In these three sentences, the varying position of **even** radically affects meaning:

4 **Even** Bert offered money.
5 Bert **even** offered money.
6 Bert offered **even money.**

Sentence 4 puts the chief stress on **Bert.** The implication is that Bert is a notorious skinflint, but that in the circumstances he is (unusually) prepared to cough up!

Sentence 5 puts the chief stress on **money**. This too *might* imply that Bert is mean; alternatively, it could signal **desperation** or **extreme determination** on his part.

Sentence 6 is both less dramatic and more technical than 4 and 5. Here Bert is a **bookmaker**, trying to deter the punters by quoting stringent odds on the favourite for the Derby/The World Cup/the next Pope/whatever.

As I said at the beginning of this chapter, all of this book has concerned itself with **syntax**, whether in terms of choosing the right word at the right time or of grammatical structures in general. Syntax is the writer's signature: like all good signatures, it should be both clear and stylishly individual. Proper attention to rudimentary sense and crisp exactness of word-order should ensure that your own 'signature' satisfies both criteria.

Chapter 5

Parts of speech (advanced)

5.1 PRELIMINARY

Chapter Two covers the eight Parts of Speech in considerable detail, but its range is restricted. Although some of the material on verbs, adjectives and adverbs looks at compounds – structures of more than one word expressing a uniform linguistic concept – on the whole its focus is on **single words**. This section is mainly devoted to the further study of compounds – phrases and clauses that do the work of verbs, nouns and so on. In addition, it covers certain other sophisticated matters 'postponed' from the earlier Chapter.

I stressed at the outset that this is not a fully comprehensive *Guide*, and I do not claim to cover every matter pertaining to Parts of Speech. But my hope is that between them Chapters Two and Five take care of most of the things that you need to know or will find useful.

5.2 VERBS

Direct and reported speech

Please read these elementary sentences:

1 I am going into town.
2 He drives like a maniac.
3 They all detest pasta.

In each case there is an implicit sense of speech: as we read we **hear** the words as well. And to make that sense of speech explicit doesn't require much effort or ingenuity:

1a 'I am going into town,' he told them
2a 'He drives like a maniac,' she observed.
3a 'They all detest pasta,' the waiter explained.[1]

It would not be quite accurate to call those examples of **dialogue**, because that word presupposes an *exchange* of speech, and the above sentences are all 'one-offs'. But the principles of dialogue are the same as exist here – indicated direct speech plus an identification of the speaker. You will of course frequently come across direct speech and dialogue in novels, short stories and several other genres, and almost certainly most of you will have had occasion to use them yourselves.

But supposing you don't want to use direct speech, or feel it is inappropriate? After all, direct speech is either taboo or irrelevant in a number of written tasks: most reportage; the writing of minutes; précis, summary and report work; reviewing; instructional and technical writing. How do you keep the **sense** of the direct speech you'd use in other circumstances while changing the **form**?

Let's return to my three examples. To put them into **reported speech** – that is, speech that you **report** rather than **quote** – is quite a complex process, even in such elementary sentences.

1b   He told them that he was going into town.
2b   She observed that he drove like a maniac.
3b   The waiter explained that they all detested pasta.

Sentence 1b changes the original **I** to **he**; 2b and 3b retain the original pronouns. But – and this is the most important feature of reported speech – all three have changed the tense of the direct speech verb. Reported speech is, as it were, one stage removed from direct speech, and this is usually reflected by moving 'one tense back'.

But not always. Before we go onto other examples, look at these versions of 2 and 3:

2c   She observed that he drives like a maniac.
3c   The waiter explained that they all detest pasta.

---

1   At this juncture the difference between writing direct speech and reported speech is my chief concern, not the mechanics and conventions of speech punctuation. I deal fully with the latter in Chapter Six.

Here the original tenses have been retained. In this form 2c and 3c suggest that what the verbs represent is a matter of **permanence** – i.e. that he always drives like a maniac and probably always will, that their detestation of pasta is unchangeable. Both notions are highly plausible, and the sentences are perfectly correct. But they are, obviously, different in meaning from 2b and 3b, and when fashioning reported speech, make sure that your version means what you really want it to.

To recast direct speech already in the past tense, follow the principle of moving back one tense. If the direct speech is in the perfect tense, use the pluperfect; if it's in the past imperfect, use the continuous pluperfect:

	Direct	**Reported**
4	'I have been out,' he admitted.	He admitted that he had been out.
5	'I have never done such a thing,' she maintained.	She maintained that she had never done such a thing.
6.	'I was going to resign,' he revealed.	He revealed that he had been going to resign.
7	'I was just having a drink,' he said.	He said that he had just been having a drink.

Notice, however, that the reported speech version of 7 is ambiguous in a way that its direct speech counterpart is not. The latter means:

All I was doing was having a drink.

But we can interpret the former in two ways:

He said that all he had been doing was having a drink.

or

He said that he had just **finished** having a drink.

Once again, you need to be completely sure that you've rendered the original accurately, both in meaning and in grammar. On this occasion, the ambiguity can be prevented by substituting **merely** for **just**:

He said that he had merely been having a drink.

Judging from the number of mistakes people make, the **simple past** tense is a misnomer when it comes to translating it into reported speech! In fact, the 'one tense back' principle still applies, but it's very easy to be careless. Study these little sentences:

8   'I was lonely,' he said.
9   'We did it,' they admitted.

In reported speech these must go into the **pluperfect**:

8a   He said that he had been lonely.
9a   They admitted that they had done it.

If you incautiously were to leave them in the **simple past**

8b   He said that he was lonely.
9b   They admitted that they did it.

you suggest that the original words were in the present:

8c   'I am lonely,' he said.
9c   'We do it,' they admitted.

So take special care!

Dealing with 'you'

So far all my examples have been in the first or third person. The second person is sometimes tricky to render in reported speech:

1   'You are ridiculous,' she remarked.
2   'Are you ready?' he asked.

As each stands, we cannot tell whether the **you** is male or female, singular or plural. Normally, the context and surrounding material should solve the problem, and you can select the appropriate pronoun:

1a   She remarked that he/she was quite ridiculous.
1b   She remarked that they were ridiculous.
2a   He asked if he/she was ready.
2b   He asked if they were ready.

However, if the context does not clarify things, you need to use an impersonal noun rather than guess at the appropriate pronoun:

1c   She remarked that the addressee was ridiculous.
2c   He asked if the auditor was ready.

Both sound pompous and awkward, I freely admit – and they are forced to choose between singular and plural. All they do is make the best of a bad job: let's hope you never have to do the same!

So far I have made no mention of future tenses and their forms in reported speech: that is because they need a section to themselves. Four modal auxiliary verbs are involved in their construction, and the function of those needs to be precisely understood before reported speech matters can be tackled.

Shall or will?

What is the difference between these four uses of the future tense?

1   I shall do the essay tomorrow evening.
2   I will do the essay tomorrow evening.
3   They will return at six o'clock.
4   They shall return at six o'clock.

Many people think that **shall** and **will** are interchangeable, but strictly speaking they are not. Moreover, the ways in which they differ are highly complicated.

In the **first person**:

I/we **shall** expresses the simple future.
I/we **will**, though still expressing the future, additionally conveys intention or determination.

Thus 1 is an unadorned statement, while 2 resembles a promise.

But the position is reversed in the **second** and **third persons**:

You, he, she, it and they **will** express the simple future.
You, he, she, it and they **shall** are almost directives. They still express the future, but there is an additional sense of determination or even command conveyed.

Thus it is 3 above that is the unadorned statement; 4 is in effect issuing an order, or at least expressing the speaker's belief that the words will come true.

All this seems somewhat pedantic, no doubt. After all, in speech and in writing we often contract these verbs, and when we do, the form is the same regardless of whether **shall** or **will** was at issue:

I'll; you'll; he'll; she'll; it'll; they'll

Given that much ordinary usage obliterates the distinction, why does it matter at all? Well, anything that preserves shades of meaning should be honoured, not out of empty reverence for the heritage of the language but because such nuances aid precision and clarity. And those who don't know or care about the difference between **shall** and **will** invariably land themselves in serious trouble when trying to render those verbs in **reported speech**, which is where their cousins **should** and **would** come in.

Should or would?

This pair of words is used in two quite separate constructions. We shall shortly see how they help form **conditional tenses**; first, a look at how they create a tense known as **the future in the past**.

The future in the past

This tense is formed when you change direct speech with a future tense verb into reported speech. Let's look again at two sentences studied earlier:

1 I shall do the essay tomorrow evening.
2 They will return at six o'clock.

These simple statements about the future are translated into reported speech form thus:

3 I said that I should do the essay tomorrow evening.
4 He said that they would return at six o'clock.

For statements about the future that additionally indicate a promise or an implied order, the procedure is different. Remember these earlier sentences?

1 I will do the essay tomorrow evening.
2 They shall return at six o'clock.

In reported speech they become:

3 I said that I would do the essay tomorrow evening.
4 He said that they should return at six o'clock.

When dealing with the future in the past, then, **shall** always becomes **should, will** always becomes **would**. However, there remains a small problem, best illustrated by a return to sentence 3:

3a I said that I should do the essay tomorrow evening.

On reflection, we can see that the sentence is ambiguous. **Should** is not only the form **shall** takes in the future in the past: it can also, independently, be synonymous with **ought to**. As a result, 3a could imply that the speaker felt under an obligation to do the essay – a different matter from a simple statement about when it would be done. If that sense of obligation is what you wish to communicate, the best thing to do is use **ought to** and leave **should** for those simple statements.

Summary

Translating direct speech into its reported form always strikes the beginner as extremely complex. It is certainly never an easy task, because it requires fiercely clear thinking: you need to be quite sure about what the original says or is seeking to say before you can render it accurately in a different form. (The same is true if you are translating reported speech 'back' into direct speech.) However, this premium on clear thinking is also to your advantage: if you take care of that adequately, the transposition should not present any problems, since the procedure is based on watertight, logical principles. Proper attention to those principles, together with a vigilant eye for any possible ambiguity, should ensure that you perform the task successfully and with a minimum of pain.

The conditional tense

This tense is similar in some ways to the subjunctive mood (see above, pp. 33–5). Both are used to refer to theoretical rather than actual states. In this pair of examples, notice the difference that changing to the conditional tense makes:

1 I **shall** react to any change in the programme with extreme disapproval.
2 I **should** react to any change in the programme with extreme disapproval.

Sentence 1 is essentially a threat. The speaker implies that such change is likely, and that he will duly complain with great vigour. Sentence 2 is markedly different in **tone**. The speaker remains firm and prepared to speak out, but his use of should implies that it will probably not be necessary: his words express the hope that wisdom will prevail and that no change will be made.

In the conditional tense, one uses **should** in the first person and **would** in the second and third persons. Thus:

3   If you cared about us, you **would** be home more often.
4   They **would** have made a mess of it regardless.

In informal and oral usage, **should** and **would** are considered interchangeable. That is comfortable and perfectly acceptable; for formal usage, however, you should attempt to stick to the rules and conventions I've outlined, mainly because not to do so will eventually, as we've seen, cause ambiguity or confusion in your writing, a blemish you should always seek to avoid.

Phrasal verbs

A phrasal verb consists of a main verb combined with another word to make a new main verb. There are three ways of forming such a structure:

A	**Verb + adverb**	take off	break down
B	**Verb + preposition**	look at	hit on
C	**Verb+adverb + preposition**	put up with	get stuck in

In all these cases, the additional word or words become part of the verb rather than operate as a separate part of speech. Thus the sentence

He got stuck into his work

consists of three basic components – subject (**He**), verb (**got stuck into**) and object (**his work**).

As that example suggests, phrasal verbs are often less complicated than they might appear. But some are transitive, others intransitive; in addition, transitive phrasal verbs can pose subtle problems of word order. Both these matters require a separate look.

Transitive and intransitive phrasal verbs

Type A (verb + adverb) can be either transitive or instransitive, as this brief list of examples shows:

Transitive	Intransitive
to break something up	to break down
to catch somebody up	to catch on
to close something down	to go away
to leave something out	to get about

Type B (verb + preposition) are always transitive.

He asked for more money.
He arrived at St. Pancras.
I believe in God.
I came across a fascinating article.

Some such verbs can be **doubly transitive**, in that both the verb and the preposition take an object:

He asked his boss for more money.
He referred the complaining woman to the manager.

Type C (verb + adverb + preposition) are also always transitive.

We are looking forward to your performance.
I am fed up with writing essays.
She walked out on him.

Note: It was with those three sentences that I ended the original (1993) incarnation of this subsection. I would not say that it was a cursory discussion, but the intervening years have suggested that it needs some expansion. The terms involved – and the need to decode them all simultaneously – have caused most of my own students noticeable difficulty, and I hope the new material which follows clears things up. It begins by revisiting two items in Exercise 4.[2]

---

2   See above, Chapter Two, p. 26.

Are these sentences featuring the verb **ran over** transitive or intransitive?

A The bulldozer ran over the hedgehog.
B The cheetah ran over the field.

A (very good) student of mine thought both were transitive. She was right about A, where the verb is a phrasal one and means 'squashed'. Here **ran over** is in effect hyphenated: **over** belongs to **ran** rather than to **hedgehog**. But this is not so in B, where the verb is simply **ran**. In this case **over** belongs to **the field**, rendering the verb *in*transitive. There is no grammatical object here: this time it is **over the field** that is in effect hypenated, forming an adverb phrase that tells us *where* **the cheetah ran.**

The best way of working out such things is to paraphrase the verb at issue. In most instances you should be able to supply a one-word synonym for it, which will quickly enable you to see whether the preposition belongs to the verb or to the words which follow it. Here are five pairs of examples with accompanying commentary.

1a He looked at me.   **Transitive**
1b He looked at ease.   **Intransitive**

In 1a the verb is **looked at**, as in 'observed': **me** is its object. In 1b, the verb is just **looked**, as in 'seemed': **at ease** tells us *how* he looked, and there is no object.

2a The carpenter drove in the nails. **Transitive**
2b The couple drove in silence.   **Intransitive**

In 2a the verb is **drove in**, as in 'implanted' or 'inserted': the object is **the nails**. In 2b the verb is simply **drove**, as in 'motored': **in silence** gives information about *how* the action was performed, and again there is no object.

3a The car operates on diesel.   **Intransitive**
3b The surgeon operated on his brain. **Transitive**

In 3a the verb is **operates**, as in 'runs': **on diesel** tells us **how** it does so, and there is no object. In 3b the verb is **operated on**, as in 'treated' or (let us hope!) 'restored': **his brain** is the object.

4a The cow jumped over the moon.   **Transitive**
4b The horses jumped over a mile.   **Intransitive**

In 4a, the verb is **jumped over**, as in 'vaulted': **the moon** is the thing thus vaulted, and so it is the object. The idea is of course preposterous, but that's how its grammar works! Sentence 4b is admittedly clumsy, but I trust it's evident that **over a mile** is a phrase informing you of the *distance of a jumping race*, not that the horses took off and soared for more than a mile before landing! Therefore the verb is just **jumped**, and there is no object.

5a Write in English.   **Intransitive**
5b Write 'in English'.   **Transitive**

An intriguing example of what a difference quotation marks can make. In 5a the order is to write in a particular *way*, again answering the question *how?* In 5b the order is to write a particular *thing*, answering the question *what?* The writer is expected to write down those words, which are therefore the object of **write**.

That last example and commentary sets up another way in which you can decode such structures. If you have a verb followed by a preposition, work out whether the latter helps to answer the question *what?* or the question *how?'*. If it's *what?*, then the preposition will 'belong' to the verb, making it a phrasal verb and what follows it the object; if it's *how?*, then the preposition will 'belong' to the words which follow, forming an adverb phrase.

Word order in transitive phrasal verbs

As I've stressed throughout this book, listening to what you write should normally allow you to achieve the best word order, in terms of both clarity and elegance. But the three types of phrasal verb are worth a detailed look in this respect, for they follow varying conventions.

Type A (verb + adverb)
If the object is a **noun**, it may appear either before the adverb or after it, as this pair of (perfectly correct) sentences demonstrates:

1   He caught up **the leader** during the final lap.
1a He caught **the leader** up during the final lap.

If the object is a **pronoun**, however, it must appear **before** the adverb:

1b   He caught him up during the final lap.[3]

Type B (verb + preposition)
No real problems here: whether noun or pronoun, the object comes after the preposition:

2   I believe in **democracy**.
2a   I believe in **it**.

But, as noted, one needs to be quite careful if a phrasal verb is used in such a way that both the root verb and the preposition take an object:

3   The secretary checked the agenda with the chairman.
3a   The secretary checked it with him.
3b   The secretary checked it with the chairman.
3c   The secretary checked the agenda with him.

Notice that the word order does not in fact change whether nouns, pronouns or a mixture of the two is used. But if my experience as a reader/marker is anything to go by, many people get into a surprising tangle with such structures, perpetrating things like

3d   The secretary checked with the chairman the agenda.
or
3e   The secretary checked with him the agenda.

Perhaps such stilted phrasing is a spin-off from the notion that one should not end sentences with prepositions or, by extension, prepositional phrases. As I've already pointed out (see pp. 2–6 and pp. 67–8) this is a mistaken belief that can often damage good English rather than guarantee it; so stick to structures 3–3c.

Type C (verb + adverb + preposition)
Apparently complicated but in fact straightforward: in every phrasal verb of this type, all parts of the verb come before the object, be it noun or pronoun:

4   Don't put up with bad manners.
4a   Don't put up with them.

3   I'm sure you can see/hear that 'He caught up him during the final lap,' is clumsy and ugly.

Phrasal verbs: a summary

Phrasal verbs are a particular kind of compound verb – that is, a verb consisting of more than one word. These can seem very forbidding, especially when they run to four, five or even six words:

1   I **have been looking forward to** your visit.   (5)
2   I **am not putting up with** this any longer.   (5)
3   He **should not have got out of** that so easily.   (6)

But I hope they seem far less formidable once you understand that even verb 3 expresses **one idea**. Remove one of the six words, or attempt to break them down into subsections, and meaning collpases. To be sure, several components and complex aspects are involved:

(a)   the subtle use of **should** in the sense of **ought to**;
(b)   a compound tense (here, the perfect);
(c)   an adverb and a preposition as part of the verb;
(d)   the addition of a negative.

Nonetheless, all four components end up doing a single job; all six words are as it were hyphenated, forming a single Part of Speech. If you are able to look at words in that **conceptual** way, and not as separate, necessarily one-off entities, these verbs should cause you minimal trouble, either in writing what you want to say or arriving at an exact understanding of others' writing.

As we get ready to focus on the noun and then on other parts of speech, an appropriate way of concluding this detailed consideration of the verb is to look at a matter that in my teaching experience is an even greater source of confusion than phrasal verbs.

The problem of words ending in -ing

No competent student has any trouble identifying *simple* (i.e. one-word) verbs – **I went, she drove, they coped** and so on – and most soon become comfortable with elementary compounds:

A *Simple*	B *Compound equivalent*
I went	I **was going** / I **have gone**
She drove	She **was driving** / She **has driven**
They coped	They **were coping** / They **have coped**

There are subtle differences in actual *meaning* between A and B there (and moreover between the two B alternatives themselves) but that is not my concern on this occasion, which is that in all three cases the **-ing** words clearly help form a verb. I covered this elementary use of the ***present participle*** in the earlier Parts of Speech chapter (p. 36) and few seem to have a problem with it.

The trouble – for both student and teacher! – is this:

> **Just because the *-ing* ending *often* denotes a compound verb does not mean that it *always* does.**

For

> **Words ending in *-ing* can also be either an *adjective* or a *noun*.**

We have looked at this before too, but experience suggests that a more detailed coverage is required. Please study these two phrases

> **the teeming rain   a crying shame**

The **-ing** words derive from verbs, certainly – **teem** and **cry**. But in this case their function is to modify (give more information about) the two nouns **rain** and **shame**, which means their function is adjectival, not verbal.

So far, so good. But what is the function of the **-ing** word in these next two examples?

> **Drinking good wine is a delight.   Flying terrifies him.**

Two sentences this time, not phrases: the verbs in question are **is** and **terrifies**. So what about the **-ing** words?

Well, as you may recall from Chapter One,[4] the technical name for them is ***gerunds***. A gerund is a ***verbal noun*** – that is a noun fashioned out of a verb. **Drinking** derives from **drink**, **flying** from **fly**. That may seem – indeed *be* – absurdly obvious. The fact remains that a lot of people find it very difficult to grasp how a word which ends in **-ing** and implies physical activity (as **flying** and **drinking** undeniably do) can possibly be a noun or indeed anything other than a verb. And I am very sympathetic

---

4   See above, 1:2, Item 12; p. 12.

to such a block: in each case the sentence conjures up a decidedly active picture – precisely the kind of thing you associate with those doing words, verbs. The solution to the block is to consider first and foremost not what the words imply or what you associate with them but what they do. At first glance **flying** and **drinking** may *seem* to be verbs but they aren't: they are the *subjects* of the verbs, and as such they can only be nouns.

So the key is to determine the exact grammatical function of a given word in its particular context. If you do that, even these further complications should not tax you overmuch. Here are two more gerunds:

> **The going was good.**   **She finished the washing.**

Both **going** and **washing** are *nouns,* respectively the subject of the verb was and the object of the verb **finished**. But in a different context they could become adjectives –

> **a going concern**   **washing powder**

– or, to return to our beginning, part of a compound verb –

> **They were going home.**   **I am washing my hair.**

In short and in summary, words ending in **-ing** can be one of three Parts of Speech, according to how and where they are used. The **-ing** ending will signify *either*

> a **participle** operating as part of a compound **verb**
> or   a **participle** operating as an **adjective**
> or   a **gerund** (= a verbal **noun**)

To conclude, try the exercise that follows, which I hope will illuminate further this trickiest of grammatical areas and help consolidate your grasp of it. After that, we move onto a further look at the noun.

Exercise 13
The bracketed figures on the right refer to the number of **-ing** words in each sentence; there are **25** in all, and your task is to identify each one as *part of a verb*, an *adjective* or a *noun*. On this occasion,

continued

> the answers do not appear in Appendix II: I feel it may be more
> helpful to provide them straightaway, so they appear below.
>
> 1 Who is going to come with me to the cinema?   (1)
> 2 I love Otto's playing – but then I am a tone-deaf moron. (1)
> 3 That woman gives me the screaming habdabs.   (1)
> 4 The running brook warbled prettily most of the time, but
>   when in flood its singing changed to a roar.   (2)
> 5 Beginning an eight-course meal is fine: it's finishing the damn
>   thing* that bothers me.   (2 + 1)
> 6 Painting the Forth Bridge is a never-ending task.   (2)
> 7 The car's main hosepipe is perishing, and so am I after trying
>   to fix it in the snow for two hours!   (2)
> 8 In Maths you get far more marks for your working than for
>   getting the right solution.   (2)
> 9 When assembling a bookcase, one overriding point is worth
>   remembering: if you are 'persuading' a shelf into its place, keep
>   your thumb out of the way of the sodding hammer.   (5)
> 10 England is not a great fielding side at present, but its batting
>   is more than all right on paper, as is its bowling. Doing it on
>   the pitch is a different matter, however: the team appears to
>   have an unerring ability to underachieve, which is a kindly
>   term for cocking things* up.   (6 + 1)
>
> * **thing / things** is not part of a verb, not an adjectival participle,
> and not a gerund. What Part of Speech *is* it?

Answers and explanations

Q number	Word	Commentary
1	going	**part of verb** 'who is going'.
2	playing	**noun**. The sense here is 'the playing of Otto'.
3	screaming	**adjective** modifying 'habdabs'.
4	running	**adjective** modifying 'brook'.
	singing	**noun**. The sense here is 'the singing of the brook'.

5	starting	**noun**. The sense here is 'the starting of the eight-course meal'.
	finishing	**noun**. The sense here is 'the finishing of the eight-course meal'.
	thing	*common/concrete noun*
6	painting	**noun**. The sense here is 'the painting of the Forth Bridge'.
	never-ending	**adjective** modifying 'task'.
7	perishing	**part of verb** '. . . hosepipe is perishing'.
	trying	noun *Very* difficult: the overwhelming temptation is to think it a verb. But 'trying' is governed by the preposition 'after', and prepositions can only govern nouns or pronouns, never verbs. *QED!*
8	working	**noun.** Governed by the adjective 'your', therefore it must be a noun – adjectives can't modify verbs!
	getting	**noun.** The sense here is 'the getting of the right solution'.
9	assembling	free-standing participle, therefore **part of a verb**.
	overriding	**adjective** modifying 'point'.
	remembering	**noun.** It could be preceded by 'the', and while 'worth the remembering' is a stilted phrase, it confirms the noun status.
	persuading	**part of verb** 'you are persuading'.
	sodding	**adjective** modifying 'hammer'.
10	fielding	**adjective** modifying 'side'.
	batting	**noun.** Preceded by the adjective 'its', and the overall sense is 'the batting of England'.
	bowling	**noun.** As for 'batting' immediately above.
	Doing	**noun.** The sense here is 'The doing of it on the pitch', however clumsy that sounds.
	unerring	**adjective** modifying 'ability'.
	cocking up	**noun.** The sense here is 'the cocking up of things'.
	things	*common/concrete noun*

5.3 NOUNS

The six classes of noun

In Chapter 2 I divided nouns into four types: concrete, proper, collective and abstract. However, that is not the full story: nouns also divide into six **classes** – a more sophisticated matter, though overlapping with that earlier material:

1   Nouns are either **proper** or **common.**
2   The latter are then further divisible into **count** and **noncount** nouns.
3   And both count and noncount nouns can then be divided into **concrete** or **abstract.**

Proper and common nouns

This first pair of classes is problematic, but not because the division itself is difficult: indeed, most pupils/students find proper nouns easy. There are two major reasons for this:

1 Proper nouns are names of specific people, places, events, publications, times and so on; as such they are always capitalised, and thus easy to recognise and use correctly.

2 The **behaviour** of proper nouns is limited and simple.
(a) They are always able to stand alone –

Washington   Whitsun   Marmaduke

– in a way denied to the majority of singular common nouns. Thus it makes perfect sense to say

(i) I found Washington frightening.
(ii) Marmaduke has caught a mouse.

but something is clearly wrong with

(iii) I found book frightening.
(iv) Cat has caught a mouse.

(b) They usually do not take a plural form. Some can –

Fridays   Christmases   Cup Finals

– but most are meaningless and unconvincing in plural form:

> Cambridges   Sallys   Niagaras

(c) They are not normally used with determiners: it is obviously absurd to speak of

> **a** Cambridge   **the** Sally   **some** Niagara

As I said in Chapter Two, I find it is the term **common noun** that causes difficulty. A formal definition might run:

> **A common noun is one which refers to something or someone as a member of the set of similar things.**

Thus a **dog** is a member of the set of all dogs. However, for the (I suspect) many people who do not find that explanation very illuminating, it's probably easier to make a virtue of the fact that proper nouns are easy to recognise and thus say:

> **All nouns that are not proper are by definition common.**

Count and noncount nouns

I don't much like these terms either, but they are useful in distinguishing between individual or countable entities –

> **books   players   desks   animals**

– and nouns that refer to an undifferentiated mass or notion:

> **milk   earth   music   luck**

If ever in doubt about whether a noun is count or noncount, try to remember these three characteristics:

1 Count nouns cannot stand alone in the singular. There is obviously something wrong with:

> **Book is damaged   animal is wounded**

2 Count nouns allow a plural; noncount nouns do not. Thus the above

books   players   desks   animals

are fine, but it sounds and looks odd to refer to

milks   earths   musics   lucks

3 Count nouns occur in the singular with the indefinite article (**a, an**), noncount nouns with **some**:

a book   an animal   some music   some luck

Both count and noncount nouns can be used with the definite article (**the**):

the book   the player   the music   the luck

Finally: quite a number of nouns can be count or noncount, according to their precise meaning or use. For example:

1a	I refuse to eat meat.	(**noncount**)
1b	There was a splendid selection of cold meats.	(**count**)
2a	I'd love some tea.	(**noncount**)
2b	Do you serve afternoon teas?	(**count**)
3a	He writes literary criticism.	(**noncount**)
3b	Do you have any specific criticisms?	(**count**)

Concrete and abstract nouns

This distinction has already been covered in detail on pp. 42–4, and not much need be added here. Abstract nouns refer to intangible items – anything that cannot be seen, heard, touched, tasted or smelled. Many are easy to recognise because they end in **-ness** –

happiness   cleanliness   ugliness   faithfulness

– but there are numerous other forms:

joy   precision   remark   intensity   evil

The key thing to bear in mind is that all abstract nouns are **mental constructs**: they are ideas, notions, judgements and so on, created by the human mind and having no physical existence. If in doubt about whether a noun is concrete or abstract, try imagining whether it could be physically isolated or transferred as an entity: could you photograph it or give it to someone? You could if it's a mountain or a sweet, but you cannot take a snapshot of music or give someone a chunk of intensity!

Gender

Many languages divide all their nouns into masculine or feminine forms. English does not do this, but there are still many occasions when gender has to be observed.

In essence, the gender of a noun is determined or signalled by the pronoun or possessive adjective that goes with it:

> I admire that **man**: **he** is superb at his job.
> **She** is a **girl** who worries too much about her weight.
> The **table** is in the wrong place: move **it**, please.
> I'm offering you some **advice** and I suggest you take **it**.

Those examples illustrate two of the three 'groups' in which gender operates – **personal animate** nouns and **inanimate** nouns. The third group, **nonpersonal animate** nouns, is used of animals and occasionally machines. An animal can of course be referred to as **it**, but most animals have specific male/female forms:

> **bull/cow   dog/bitch   cock/hen   cob/pen   dog/vixen**

'Lower' animals and fish (e.g. flies, ants, plaice) are not distinguished in such a way, however.

One of the more delightful – or ridiculous, according to your point of view – eccentricities of English is its tendency to give cars, aeroplanes, ships and the like the **feminine** gender:

> **She** is a lovely car – fast and elegant.
> The plane was damaged but the pilot landed **her** safely.

Personally I have a lot of sympathy with the character in Ian Fleming's short story *The Hildebrand Rarity* who responds thus to James Bond's remark 'She's your ship':

It's my ship . . . That's another bit of damned nonsense, making a hunk of steel and wood female.'[5]

He seems to be in a minority, however; such practice, sentimental nonsense or not, is still widespread, and you should bear it in mind. In addition, countries are often referred to in the feminine form, despite some nations' fondness for the term '**Father** land'.

5.4 ADJECTIVES AND ADVERBS

The articles

There are two kinds of article – **definite** and **indefinite**.

definite article   =   **the**
indefinite article =   **a, an**

The terms may seem rather imposing for words that are the simplest adjectives of all. But articles are far from inconsequential: their omission can make a significant difference to meaning.

1   **A man** walked into the shop.
2   **Man** is the most recent of the planet's species.
3   Pass me **the books**, please.
4   **Books** are amongst life's greatest treasures.

In 1 and 3 the highlighted articles make their nouns **specific**, whereas in 2 and 4 the absence of an article makes the nouns **general** or **universal**. All four are quite correct; but when writing, stay alert to whether you need an article or not. **The** and **a/an** may not seem to matter much one way or another, but they are crucial aids to precision and do a surprising amount of work.

Adjective order

On the whole it is not good writing practice to string together a lot of adjectives: even three will often seem excessive, let alone six or seven!

5   In *For Your Eyes Only* (Pan, 1962), p.163.

But on those occasions when you do employ several determiners at once, you should follow this order:

1	Adjectives describing **feelings** or **qualities**	(pleasant)
2	Adjectives of **size, age, temperature**, or **measurement**	(big, young, cold)
3	Adjectives of **colour**	(pink)
4	Adjectives of **nationality** or **origin**	(Welsh)
5	Adjectives denoting **substance** or **material**	(iron, linen)

Thus:

(a)   I met a **pleasant young black American** miner.

(b)   She bought a **large old Irish linen** tablecloth.

I hope you agree, however, that those examples are dangerously top-heavy; such four-adjective constructions should be kept to an absolute minimum.

When adjectives precede the noun, you do not need separating commas, as (a) and (b) illustrate; neither should you normally use **and**, except for adjectives of **colour**:

The large **red and white** linen tablecloth.

Certain adjectives cannot precede nouns:

asleep   afraid   afloat   alive   alone

It sounds (indeed **is**) wrong to say:

the asleep boy   I saw an afloat body

You need to change either the construction or the adjective:

the boy was asleep   or   the **sleeping** boy
I saw a body afloat   or   I saw a **floating** body

Further matters of order and punctuation

One of the commonest errors in both speech and writing follows this kind of pattern:

As a novelist, she admires Hardy, but not as a man.

That sentence does not actually say what it intends: **as a novelist** goes with **she**, not **Hardy**. That's perfectly possible, of course – she could very well be a novelist herself – but it's obviously ridiculous to imagine that she can also operate **as a man**, which is what must be implied if that first interpretation is maintained! The sentence suffers from a '**hanging**' **descriptor** or **displaced nominative** – two perhaps rather stuffy terms that we encountered in Chapter One.[6] In practice, they merely indicate that the words need to be better arranged:

> She admires Hardy as a novelist but not as a man.

Taking real care over such matters will bring two benefits. First, it will mean that you're in no danger of looking or sounding foolish! This is less trivial than it might seem: time after time I'm irritated by male interviewers who say to their female guests

> As a woman, I'd like to ask you . . .

to the extent that I fail to concentrate on the question that follows. That may be just silly of me, but I know that many other people react in a similar way, and such moments are not conducive to good communication.

Second, and more important, it will prevent ambiguity. For displaced nominatives can lead to weightier problems than mere absurdity, as a return to a shortened version of that first example shows:

> As a novelist, she admires Hardy.

Strictly speaking, this can only mean that **she** is a novelist herself. But, as noted, that may not be the meaning that is intended; furthermore, even if that meaning is intended, many readers whether they be ignorant, unalert or suspicious are likely to assume the alternative. You may think that you've got quite enough to take care of without legislating for bad or suspicious readers, and I very much see your point. However, in this case the solution is simple. When using a descriptor like 'as a novelist' or whatever, try this little test:

> **If you immediately add the relevant reflexive pronoun (myself, herself, etc.), will the sentence still make sense?**

6   See Exercise 1 above, p. 6, item 26.

For example:

A (Male) 'As a woman **myself**, may I ask you . . .'
   The addition immediately confirms the absurdity; the descriptor is
   obviously in the wrong place.
B (Pianist) 'As an instrument **myself**, I prefer the Steinway.'
   As for A.
C (Pianist) 'As a pianist **myself**, I prefer the Steinway.'
   Perfectly correct, and clear.
D (Novelist) 'As a novelist **myself**, I admire Hardy.'
   As for C.
E (Non-writing reader) 'As a novelist **myself**, I admire Hardy.'
   Less absurd than A and B, perhaps, but it still won't do.

That test, then, will instantly help you to diagnose the accuracy or
otherwise of what you're planning to say. And if you do intend the kind
of meaning illustrated by C and D, it is good policy to include the
reflexive pronoun in your written phrase, if only to dispel suspicious
readers' doubts that you really mean what you say.

Finally, remember always to punctuate with absolute precision, especially
when you employ **relative** adjectives. Consider the difference in meaning
between these two sentences, which follow the pattern first explored on
p. 54.

1   The book, which is expensive, is essential reading.
2   The book which is expensive is essential reading.

One means that a specific book is expensive but must be read. Two means
that **any** book that happens to be expensive must be read – a clearly
preposterous idea. As we recently found when looking at the definite and
indefinite articles, small and apparently inconsequential omissions or
inclusions can make a very big difference.

5.5 ADVERB CLAUSES

Just as there are many types of one-word or phrasal adverbs, so there are
many varieties of adverb clauses. We all use them every day, naturally
and unthinkingly, and becoming fully aware of what they are and how
they work is less difficult than you might imagine. They are always

prefaced by a **conjunction** – which makes them tolerably easy to recognise. In addition, adverb clauses are always **subordinate**: in every example given below, the clause in bold type either introduces the main statement or completes it.

In all there are nine kinds of adverb clause.[7] I believe the first three are sufficiently straightforward to speak for themselves, but I've provided some further explanation for the remaining six.

Types of conjuction

1   **Time**   *when, before, after, while, since, till, until,*
                                as, as soon as

When I've finished this essay, I shall go out.
He hasn't seen her **since they went to a May Ball together.**
I can't comment **until I've seen the Report.**
As they pass by, pluck Casca by the sleeve. (*Julius Caesar*)

2   **Place**   *where, wherever*

Fools rush in **where angels fear to tread.**
Where there's a will there's a way.
Wherever you see flowers you'll find insects too.

3   **Degree or Comparison**   *as, than*

Few men worked harder **than did J. P. Morgan.**
She is as wise **as she is beautiful.**
He is taller **than his brother was at his age.**

4   **Cause**   *because, for, since, as*

Since there's no help, let us kiss and part. (Michael Drayton)
As he was unqualified, he did not expect a large salary.
I dislike him **because he is arrogant.**

---

7   The classification I have used derives largely from the splendid *Report on Grammatical Terminology*, a pre-Second World War publication that in many respects has never been bettered.

For obvious reasons, Type 4 is easy to recognise when the relevant conjunction is **because**. It is trickier if **since** is involved: as we've already seen, that conjunction can also introduce an adverb clause of **time**. That is also true of **as**, which is trickier still, since it can also introduce adverb clauses of **comparison** and **manner**. This is unlikely to be a problem when *writing*; however, as I remarked in the Preface, a sure grasp of grammar can greatly improve the efficiency and perception of your **reading**. The correct identification of **as** here is a case in point, essential if one is to be sure of understanding the overall meaning correctly.

5   **Purpose**   *that, so that, in order that; lest* (negative)

> I shouted **that the lifeboat might hear me.**
> He smiled broadly **so that she could see he was pleased.**
> She took an umbrella **lest it rained.**

Although Type 5 is in the main problem-free, *reader-care* is needed over **so that**. In this sentence it clearly denotes intention (**purpose**) –

> He ran quickly **so that** he could catch the train.

– but not in this one:

> He ran **so** quickly **that** no one could catch him.

Here the construction **so . . . that** introduces an adverb clause of **result** – our next Type.

6   **Result**   *so . . . that*

> She took so long to get ready **that he fell asleep.**
> Many programmes are so awful **that it's not worth turning on the set.**

As noted, the only problem seems to be distinguishing between **result** and **purpose**. There are two things that may help. First, Type 6 always 'splits' the **so** and the **that**, which should make it easier to tell them apart. Second, try substituting the clause concerned with a phrase beginning **in order to**. If that substitution makes sense, then it's a clause of **purpose**; if it doesn't, or if it clearly alters the original meaning, then it's a clause of **result**. We can test that on the first example offered for each type:

5   I shouted **that the lifeboat might hear me**
              becomes
    I shouted **in order to make the lifeboat hear me.**

No observable change in sense; therefore confirmed as **purpose.**

6   She took so long to get ready **that he fell asleep.**
              becomes
    She took so long to get ready **in order to make him fall asleep.**

That isn't quite nonsense, but what is suggested is most unlikely, confirming the original clause as one of **result.**

However, if those do not entirely solve the problem, you may need to do a little lateral thinking, looking beyond the immediate grammar of the structures in question and at the larger context instead. The example I offer is rather a grand one, but it perfectly illustrates the difference between **purpose** and **result.**

In Book IX of Milton's *Paradise Lost*, Adam and Eve have a suitably epic argument about how best to fulfil their God-appointed work in the Garden of Eden. Her suggestion, 'Let us divide our labours' is countered by his concern that separation could prove calamitous, for he has earlier been warned that 'the malicious Foe' (Satan) could at any time be 'nigh at hand'. Across some two hundred lines of sublime verse that combines high comedy with intimations of even higher tragedy, their debate inexorably degenerates into the equivalent of a full-blooded marital row. Adam knows (as does the reader) that he should put his foot down, but he doesn't, preferring to sulk: his dismissive 'Go; for thy stay, not free, absents thee more'[8] sets up the climactic meeting with the Serpent/Satan, which of course leads to the Fall of Man.

The crux here, memorably pointed out by a student in one of my classes a few years ago, is that Eve does not leave Adam *in order to bring about the Fall.* That catastrophe is the **result** of her action, not its **purpose.** She is devoted to him and their life in the Garden; her desire for separation is partly a matter of practical wisdom and partly the (not unreasonable) wish for a little time to herself. Because we know what will happen when she does move away from his side, there is a temptation to

---

8   A formal translation might run: 'Go then, for if you stay against your will, that's more painful than your absence.' A much looser but still tonally apposite version might be, 'Well, sod off, then: if you don't want to stay, I don't want you here anyway, so there!'

regard the Fall not only as inevitable but as *her* fault, her sin, even her evil *intention*. That latter 'angle' may characterise some versions of the myth, but not Milton's: in *Paradise Lost* Adam is as much to blame as Eve and arguably more culpable.

And so, to return to mundane grammatical matters, it would be quite wrong to summarise that episode using an adverb clause of **purpose**:

> Eve is determined to go off on her own **so that the Fall may take place.**

It can only be expressed using an adverb clause of **result**:

> Eve is **so** determined to go off on her own **that the Fall takes place.**

Grammar always serves context; sometimes it can be useful to remember that a sense of context can help you determine how that grammar works.

7	**Condition**	*if, whether . . . or, in case, so long as, provided; unless* (negative)

> Pigs might fly **if they had wings.**
> **Whether or not you pass** depends on your coursework.
> ˙I don't care what you wear **so long as you turn up.**
> **Provided it stays fine**, we'll eat outside.
> I won't go **unless you do too.**

On the basis of those illustrations, you might think that Type 7 is one of the easier ones to identify, and I hope you indeed find that to be the case. But I have seen many students confuse clauses of **condition** with the forthcoming Type 8, **concession**. Perhaps it's the 'C-words' themselves that cause the problem, being both similar and difficult; perhaps it's the fact that both can include **if**. I go fully into this confusion – and into ways to solve it – after the next set of examples.

8	**Concession**	*although, though, even if, whatever*

> **Though I give my body to be burned**, it profiteth me nothing. (St Paul)
> **Although you have done well**, you can do better still.
> Don't look down **whatever you do.**
> **Even if you fail**, it's worth attempting it.

I can easily see why someone might think that those sentences exemplify **condition**. But all four have a decidedly negative tinge to them – and that's why dwelling on the word **concession** itself might help. It derives from **concede**, which is what you do if you admit defeat, acknowledge a superior point or argument, or even allow someone something (as in 'concede a putt' in golf). Those sentences all take a step back, so to speak – whereas the first four illustrations for Type 7 above have a more positive feel to them. The matter is admittedly complicated further by the fifth example offered, introduced by **unless**: that has a more negative impact. Perhaps the answer – if you're in need of one – is to concentrate on the **conjunctions** involved in each case: learn those and distinguishing between the two types should become easier.

9   **Manner**   *as, as if, as though*

> **As ye sow**, so shall ye reap.
> He behaved **as if he were guilty**.
> They were drinking **as though there were no tomorrow**.

Along with **time** and **place**, the adverb clause of **manner** is the most frequently encountered. It should not cause too many problems if you remember that it always answers the question 'How?'; applying that test should prevent any confusion with other types of adverb clause that employ **as**.

That concludes this survey of some of the more sophisticated properties of parts of speech. Before moving on to the section on punctuation, try the summarising exercise that follows.

Exercise 14

A   Identify the following sentences as **simple**, **double**, **multiple** or **complex**.

1   The man in the threadbare stained raincoat fell over.
2   As the boy had only just begun his apprenticeship, he did not expect high wages.
3   I love you and I need you.
4   He stood up, stretched vigorously, and then sat down hurriedly, feeling dizzy.

---

continued

B Put the following pieces of dialogue into **reported speech**.

1   'You look very ill,' she told her husband.
2   'I was just going to call the police,' he said.
3   'She was here yesterday,' the supervisor admitted.
4   'I'll be with you in a minute, sir,' the assistant promised.

C What is the difference in meaning/tone here?

1   I shall be happy just to survive.
2   I should be happy just to survive.

D Which of these are **count nouns**, and which **noncount nouns**? (NB: some might be both.)

1	Television	2	Earth	3	Courage	4	Carpet
5	Machine	6	Light	7	Record	8	Glass

E Which of these structures is correct, and which faulty?

1   As a reptile, I find the crocodile uniquely ugly.
2   As a woman, he wanted to sleep with her.
3   As a boss, he was superb; as a friend, he was worthless.
4   As a dishwasher, I think it is poorly marketed.

F Pick out the adverb clauses in these sentences and identify their type – **manner, place, time, degree/comparison, cause, purpose, result, condition** or **concession**.

1   Her hair shone as does the sun.
2   You won't survive unless you have immediate treatment.
3   The secretary carefully filed the papers so that they could be easily found.
4   I'll be pleased if it rains.
5   That orange and brown tie is quite fetching, even though at first sight it looks loathsome.
6   Some people are so lazy that they will not even answer urgent letters.
7   Where the bee sucks, there suck I.
8   As you've been under a lot of strain, we'll overlook your error this time.
9   Practise that piece in the way I showed you.

Answers are in Appendix II.

Chapter 6

Punctuation
Speech and quotation

6.1 PRELIMINARY

Why have such a chapter in a book on grammar? After all, punctuation is normally considered a discrete skill: in the main it orchestrates meaning rather than defines it, and that's why I haven't included a separate chapter on 'ordinary' punctuation.[1] However, we have already seen a number of instances where punctuation *does* influence meaning, and that is regularly an issue when it comes to punctuating speech and quotation.

A second consideration is that these skills are extremely tricky, even for fully competent writers. Contrary to many students' beliefs and practice, punctuating dialogue or quotation is **not** just a matter of providing inverted commas at appropriate places: all the other 'normal' punctuation skills remain in play as well. This means that at any one time there is a great deal to remember, a great deal to get right; and if those 'normal' skills are not fully assured, any attempt to deal with more sophisticated tasks is very likely to dissolve into chaos. And that apparently forbidding observation leads me a third reason for including this chapter. For I have found it be an almost invariable law that

> **Anyone who can punctuate speech and quotation correctly is entirely competent not only in all other aspects of punctuation but in all significant matters of grammar as well.**

In other words, if you can master this section, you can master anything.

---

1 Those who might require such a guide are referred to Part Two of the revised (2002) edition of my *Write In Style*.

6.2 PUNCTUATING SPEECH: THE RUDIMENTS

1 Practically everyone knows that punctuating speech requires the use of inverted commas. You can use either single or double inverted commas:

1a 'I'm going out now,' he said.
1b "I'm going out now," he said.

Both these versions are correct. Most publishing houses use the single version, but you are free to choose whichever one seems most natural to you. However, you should bear these two points in mind:

> *Never* mix single and double inverted commas.
> Whichever form you choose for punctuating speech, you should use the *other* one for quotation.

Following that convention will assist clarity anyway, and it is **essential** for those occasions when you need to signify a quotation within a passage of speech. This trickiest of all punctuational skills is covered later, but you can make a sound start by firmly establishing which form you will use for each mode.

2 Choosing your form of inverted commas and following it consistently is important, but it's also very straightforward. Other rudimentary matters are more problematic, as a return to that first example immediately illustrates:

1a 'I'm going out now,' he said.

Please note the highlighted comma. In my experience as a teacher, at least 90 per cent of learning students fail to insert any punctuation between the passage of speech and the other components of the narrative. **Such punctuation is mandatory at all times**, whether the speech is in the form of a statement –

1a 'I'm going out now,' he said.

– an exclamation –

1b 'I'm going out now!' he yelled.

– or a question –

1c 'May I go out now?' he asked.

In addition, if the overall structure of speech + back-up narrative **ends**
with the speech component, a full stop will be required if a statement is
involved:

1d He said, 'I'm going out now.'

Of those four examples, it is 1a and 1d that occasion the most frequent
errors. A lot of writers comfortably observe the principle behind 1b and
1c: they can 'hear' the exclamation or the question and realise it must be
drawn attention to. But those same writers are not aware of any 'break'
between 'he said' and the statement itself and punctuate (or **non-**
punctuate!) accordingly.

I am very sympathetic about this: the need for punctuation is **not**
obvious, and including it seems to serve no obvious or clarifying purpose.
The fact is that the two components of the complete structure – speech
and what I've just termed 'back-up narrative' – **are** separate, and a visual
signal is needed to register that separateness. It may not seem to matter
much in the case of the short example we've been considering; in longer
passages the need to distinguish visually between direct speech and other
writing becomes more pressing:

> 'I'm going out now,' he said, 'and I don't know when I'll be back.'
> He looked around the room. 'Where are my keys? I thought I left
> them on that table. Ah! Here they are – in my hand.' Grinning
> sheepishly, he opened the front door, muttering, 'I must be going
> ga-ga.'

That little passage is quite complex. The reader has to absorb various
remarks, and also various actions. Yes, they all go together; but I'm sure
you can see that if the 'normal' punctuation were omitted – or even just
some of it – your sense of what's being said and what's being done would
quickly get blurred. And in any extended passage of dialogue-plus-action
(involving, say, two or three speakers and a lot of accompanying
narrative) you would be quite lost within a page or so if those ordinary
punctuation conventions were ignored.

3 We'll return to those issues shortly; another rudimentary point needs to be stressed first. Look again at our 'root example':

1a 'I'm going out now,' he said.

I've already asked you to note the comma; please also note that it is placed **inside** the speech-mark. This again is standard unvarying practice, and you should commit it to memory as quickly as possible. Many people mistakenly place such punctuation **outside** the speech marks or, even worse, **directly underneath** them. The latter practice is virtually always a simple case of 'bet-hedging': the writer isn't sure where the ordinary punctuation should be placed, so tries to keep all options open! I'm afraid it does not convince: don't do it.

If you think all this is mere pedantry, it isn't: when **quoting**, your 'normal' punctuation will nearly always be placed **outside** the inverted commas. As we'll see, it can sometimes be crucial to distinguish between something that has been said or asked and something which has been quoted: the conventions I've just outlined allow you to do this clearly and with a minimum of fuss.

4 The final rudimentary point concerns **layout**. Probably the easiest way of determining how to set out exchanges of direct speech is to pick up a novel in which you know there's a lot of dialogue, find an appropriate passage and study its format. You should quickly become aware that

Each new passage of speech is indented.

And, implicit in that first principle but worth stressing on its own:

Each time the speaker changes, **a new line/paragraph is required.**

Two important considerations lie behind these principles, as this brief passage, **incorrectly** set out, illustrates:

'Where are you going to, my pretty maid?' 'Mind your own business, you sexist oaf!' 'There's no need to be like that – I was only trying to be friendly.' 'Oh yeah?' 'Yes.' 'Oh well, in that case, I'm off to a meeting of my local "Emma" group.' '"Emma"?' '"Emma", yes: "Extermination of Molesting Males Association".'

That is a bare six lines, but I'd be surprised if you found it easy going. As a single block of prose it is visually taxing: there are a great number of signals to absorb, and it becomes progressively harder to work out who is saying what. As I've stressed throughout, all good writing makes life as comfortable as possible for the reader; that passage does not make comfort a priority – and you can imagine what it might be like to read several pages similarly set out.

Happily, it is easily put right.

> 'Where are you going to, my pretty maid?'
> 'Mind your own business, you sexist oaf!'
> 'There's no need to be like that – I was only trying to be friendly.'
> 'Oh yeah?'
> 'Yes.'
> 'Oh well, in that case, I'm off to a meeting of my local "Emma" group.'
> '"Emma"?'
> '"Emma", yes: "Extermination of Molesting Males Association".'

That is much easier to take in; in addition, in this form the exchanges somehow acquire greater flow and bite. You'll notice that the correct format is not unlike a playscript: perhaps that explains the added drama of the amended passage.

You'll also notice that the acronym 'Emma' and the final explanation of its meaning are placed within **double** inverted commas. These instances are not quotations as such, but they are analogous to quotations in that they need to be highlighted, and highlighted in a clearly separate way from ordinary speech marks. More on this shortly.

The other great advantage of that correct format, implicit in those exchanges, can be deduced from reading this next passage. What's wrong with it, do you think?

> 'What's going on here?' demanded Susan.
> 'Nothing much,' replied Frank.
> 'Oh really?' she countered. 'There are three empty gin bottles on the floor, ash all over the carpet, and you seem to have forgotten to put a shirt on.'
> 'Can't a man relax after a hard day's work?' he asked.
> 'If this is relaxing,' she snapped, 'I'd hate to see what you could manage when really making an effort. And there's another thing,' she added.
> 'What?' he enquired.

'I don't seem to be able to get into our bedroom,' she informed him.

'Well,' he explained, 'you know how that door's always sticking. Damp, I expect,' he suggested. 'You really need to give it a good shove,' he continued.

'Don't give me that!' she retorted. 'It's *you* I need to give a good shove,' she went on, 'out of my house and out of my life!'

This is far from bad writing, but it's *flabby* – and in a precise way:

Apart from from the first two remarks, all the 'back-up' identifiers are unnecessary and cumulatively irritating.

Those first two lines establish situation and personnel: it's a row between Susan and Frank. Because only two speakers are involved, and because a new paragraph occurs each time the speaker changes, the reader simply doesn't need the successive **she countered, he asked, she snapped** and so on. Furthermore, they start to get in the way, to interrupt a fast-developing storm: by the time we read the final exchange, the five verbs **he explained, he suggested, he continued, she retorted** and **she went on** are mere annoying hiccups. Susan's last remarks are a scream of rage and frustration, delivered in a single breath: to chop them up like that up seriously reduces their impact.

Be sparing with 'identifiers', therefore. Of course, if your passage of dialogue involves **more** than two speakers, you'll need to make it clear who is saying which lines. This can be done through style alone – establishing a particular 'voice' or idiom for each of several speakers – but that takes a lot of practice, and straightforward identification is probably your best course for a while. In addition, there will be times when even if your dialogue is restricted to two speakers, you'll want to include back-up material in the form of qualifiers or narrative information, as in this amended extract from that last passage:

'I don't seem to be able to get into our bedroom.' She delivered each word as if biting on a stick of celery.

'Well,' he mumbled, not looking at her, 'you know how that door's always sticking.' A thought seemed to strike him. 'Damp, I expect. You really need to give it a good shove . . .'

'Don't give me that! It's *you* I need to give a good shove – out of my house and out of my life!' She flung the car-keys at his face, catching him in the left eye, and stormed out of the room.

Even here, however, the additional material is decidedly *secondary*. None of it is useless; but Frank's explanation is so intrinsically feeble that we can sense without being told that he cannot meet her eye and that he's desperately improvising. Similarly, the last sentence only makes **ex**plicit the violence **im**plicit in Susan's words throughout. So when writing dialogue, give maximum attention to **voice**: you'll be surprised and delighted to find how much unnecessary other work it can save you.

That completes this introductory look at speech-punctuation. There are further, subtle things to say about the topic, but first it is time to concentrate on punctuating quotation.

6.3 THE RUDIMENTS OF PUNCTUATING QUOTATION

1 Quotation is the exact citing of someone else's words. Its most obvious instances are those where the words are famous, and they should be 'clothed' in double inverted commas:

> "To be or not to be: that is the question."   (*Hamlet*)

> "It is a truth universally acknowledged, that a single man in possession of a good fortune, must be in want of a wife."
> (Jane Austen, *Pride and Prejudice*)

> "Let them eat cake."   (Marie Antoinette)

2 However, quotation is not **just** a matter of repeating a well-known phrase or saying. Look at these sentences:

1 'James said, "I'm fed up",' John recalled.
2 'She said, "Tell the kids I expect their rooms to be tidy when I get back",' their father told them.

These specimens of quotation may be mundane, but they're also pretty complex in terms of mechanics and design – far more so than their famous counterparts above. Let's examine in detail how each one works.

In 1 two speakers are involved – John and James. The latter's words were **I'm fed up**, and John is reporting them. All obvious enough; yet see what a difference in meaning results if we omit those double inverted commas:

1a 'James said I'm fed up,' John recalled.

Instead of a quotation, we have a form of reported speech. Here John is recalling that James said he, John, is fed up. James's remark has changed from a statement about himself to a deduction about John – a notable difference.

If we wanted to preserve the original meaning but use the reported speech mode, we would need to write:

1b 'James said that he was fed up,' John recalled.

This is perfectly satisfactory, of course. But the original achieves the same effect simply by the addition of a pair of double inverted commas – clear, compact and stylish.

Sentence 2 is longer and apparently trickier; in fact, it's more straightforward, because no potential ambiguity can arise. Again, there are two speakers – the father and an unspecified female. This time, however, the audience is implicitly identified – **the kids**, which presumably makes the female speaker their mother. If we omit the double inverted commas –

2a 'She said, tell the kids I expect their rooms to be tidy when I get back,' their father told them.

– we do not change the meaning: we just end up with something inadequately punctuated. But if you think that doesn't matter much, I hope 1 has shown you that the lazy or incautious omission of quotation marks can make a crucial difference, so be meticulous at all times!

3 When quoting, you need to be especially careful about the accompanying 'ordinary' punctuation. Take another look at that familar sentence:

'James said, "I'm fed up",' John recalled.

Please note the **order** of the highlighted punctuation:

A The closing quotation marks.
B The ordinary punctuation. (In this case a comma, but in other instances it could be a full stop, a question mark or an exclamation mark.)
C The closing speech mark.

Ordinary punctuation is nearly always placed **outside** the quotation marks. The only exception to this is if that ordinary punctuation is itself part of the quotation:

1 'What is the meaning of "acerbic"?' Simon asked.
2 The teacher commented, 'It's amazing how many people misunderstand the line, "Wherefore art thou, Romeo?"'

In 1 the question mark does not belong to **acerbic**: it signifies that Simon is asking a question about that word. But in 2 the question mark is part of the quotation, which is in the form of a question, whereas the teacher is making a statement. Therefore, the question mark belongs **inside** the quotation marks; and since the overall structure ends there, all that is needed thereafter is the closing speech-mark.

This is a sophisticated matter, often a question of taste rather than an unvarying rule: I have found that different publishers and editors adopt differing practices, according to their 'house style'.

4 It ought to be obvious that quotation marks **advertise** a quotation neatly and on their own. But many people think it is also necessary to preface any such citation with the phrase **and I quote**. When talking, the phrase is useful (though not essential), because the listener cannot, obviously, hear the quotation marks. But when writing, it is unnecessary and irritating: don't do it.

5 Finally, read this little story – an old joke (somewhat cleaned up!) that illustrates very well the rudimentary principles we've been considering. The scene is a court of law.

'Where were you on the night of the 15th June?' asked the prosecution.
'At home,' replied the vicious-looking witness.
'I see. "At home", you say. Not waiting outside the Midland Bank in a dark blue van with the engine running?'
'No way, chief.'
'And what were you doing "at home"?'
'Sod-all.'
'I'm sorry,' interrupted the judge, 'I didn't catch that last remark.'
'He said "Sod-all", m'lud,' the Clerk of the Court supplied.
'Oh, really?' said the judge. 'Funny – I thought he said something.'

I hope that amused you, and I'm sorry to descend to an analysis of it – the surest way ever devised of killing a joke. But the confusion here stems from the judge's failure to realise that the Clerk of the Court's use of 'sod-all' was a quotation, not a curt statement. The reader **does** realise this, and does so before the judge makes his remark. Hence the laughter (I hope!).

6.4 FURTHER POINTS AND FINAL REMINDERS

Early on I stressed that the inverted commas used for identifying speech or quotation are **additional** to 'normal' punctuation, not replacements for it. You must especially be on your guard when writing passages of conversation, which are likely to require a great deal of 'normal' punctuation. For conversations feature a lot of idiomatic English and interjections or similar phrases, which must all be 'signalled' clearly.

In this example the punctuation isn't all that bad; I've certainly seen worse. It's properly set out, with a new line each time the speaker changes; and the writer has remembered to include a 'normal' punctuation point after each spoken part, correctly placed inside the speech marks. Nevertheless there are several omissions and at least four choices that could be improved upon. Can you identify them?

Exercise 15

'Oh hello Mum,' George said nervously. 'Ken and I are just off to the,'

'Oh no you're not my lad,' she interrupted. 'There's the little matter of your room to tidy up and then the shoes to clean which you've been promising to do for days.'

'But Mum,' he began.

'But nothing George. You don't go out till you've done both jobs okay.'

Now study this 'fair copy' version and see how it compares with what you spotted; numbers on the right refer to the explanations below.

'Oh, hello, Mum,' George said nervously. 'Ken and I   (1)
are just off to the . . .'   (2)

'Oh no, you're not, my lad,' she interrupted.   (3)
'There's the little matter of your room to tidy up; and   (4)
then the shoes to clean which you've been promising to
do for days.'
   'But, Mum . . .' he began.   (5)
   '"But" nothing, George. You don't go out until (1; 6)
you've done both jobs, okay?'   (7)

1 **Oh, hello** and **Mum** are three separate components and must be punctuated as such. Of course, they are closely related; but they are grammatically distinct – the first two are interjections, the third a name. To be fair, only a pedant would insist on the comma between **oh** and **hello** (though it is correct); but a comma between **hello** and **Mum** is obligatory. The same goes for **nothing** and **George** further down.

2 George's sentence is unfinished: we never find out **where** Ken and he were off to, because he is **interrupted** by his mother. When dialogue is broken into in this way, you should signal it with ellipsis (. . .) – the comma merely confuses and thus won't do.

3 As for 1. Again, the comma after **no** is arguably optional, but the one after **not** is essential.

4 In my view the two chores – room tidying and shoe cleaning – need to be separated; hence the semi-colon, although a comma would do. It might be your opinion that George's mother is pretty angry and delivers the whole sentence in a breathless rush. If so, fine: keep it as it was. If, however, you think her tone is one of no-nonsense firmness, then that additional signal is necessary.

5 As for 2. Notice that the use of ellipsis means that you can, if you like, scrap **he began**: that information is *included* in those dots.

6 Putting 'But' into quotation marks is perhaps rather pedantic: I wouldn't insist on it. But it is strictly correct: she is 'throwing back' the word at him, and the extra punctuation underlines that fact.

7 Whether you insert a punctuation point between **jobs** and **okay** depends entirely on what you think to be the sentence's meaning. If you think **okay** is an adverb that goes with **done**, that George's mother is demanding that both jobs be done in a satisfactory manner, then the

Listen to what you're writing.

original version is correct as it stands. But if you take **okay** to mean something like 'Do you understand?' or 'Have you got me?', then additional punctuation is required. The comma I've chosen is accurate, but a full stop would perhaps be better if you think **okay** is delivered with a lot of top-spin or menace!

Finally, I must again stress that if you really **listen** to what you're writing, a lot of these subtle, intricate matters will occur to you almost as a matter of course. All those seven points I've listed and discussed are matters of **voice**: once you can hear what's truly being said, everything else should fall naturally into place.

Conclusion

As an exemplar of that last point and many others, please read this short extract from P. G. Wodehouse's *The Mating Season*, where Bertie Wooster

is talking about Jeeves's uncle, a formidable butler named Silversmith.
As you'll see, it is also suggested as an exercise.

Exercise 16

If you've ever found punctuating dialogue and quotation problematic, you could do worse than learn this brief passage off by
heart.

'Does Silversmith minister to the revellers at the morning
meal?'
'Yes, sir.'
'My God!' I said, paling beneath the tan. 'What a man,
5   Jeeves!'
'Sir?'
'Your Uncle Charlie.'
'Ah, yes, sir. A forceful personality.'
'Forceful is correct. What's that thing of Shakespeare's
10   about someone having an eye like Mother's?'
' "An eye like Mars, to threaten and command", is possibly
the quotation for which you are groping, sir.'

In its compact dozen lines that passage exemplifies most of the principles
and techniques I've been conerned with; I would draw particular attention to lines 8 and 11, where an incautious writer might have omitted
important commas or the quotation marks. As it is, the meticulously
correct punctuation helps voice and meaning, thus guaranteeing the
lively flow that Wodehouse intended.

There is no more concentrated writing skill than punctuating speech
and quotation, especially when they occur together; as I said at the outset,
if you can master all its intricacies, you should hardly ever make a mistake
of *any* kind.

Chapter 7

Finale

Some additional gaps and traps

7.1 PRELIMINARY

This is not the 'miscellany of afterthoughts' it might appear but a convenient way of focusing on a number of specific items that have nothing obvious in common apart from the fact that they cause trouble to many. We begin by looking further at something I described in Chapter One as 'almost certainly the most abused, least understood device in the entire spectrum of English punctuation and grammar.'

7.2 MORE ON THE APOSTROPHE

Two quick reminders:

1   All apostrophes denote the omission of a letter or letters. And so
    . . .
2   . . . It is incorrect to talk of 'the possessive apostrophe', since the 's construction at issue signifies the dropping of the e from the still-surviving genitive case.

You may think I'm in danger of becoming obsessive about Point 2: that is at least the third time it has appeared. I've been at pains to stress it not just because it's important in its own right: ignorance of that derivation leads to widespread apostrophe-abuse. Let's see how.

Apostrophe abuse

1   The apostrophe must not be used as an alternative spelling of ordinary plurals.

Despite the thousands of instances you will see in shops, on menus, in newspaper headlines and on television, it is illiterate to write such alleged plurals as:

Apple's 25p a pound.   Please close all **door's** after you.
Do you like **egg's**?   **Doctor's** get pay rise

It is easy to laugh at such wrong practice (irreverently termed 'greengrocer plurals') but it can infect even able writers. It arises, I believe, from a state of mind that automatically inserts an apostrophe before *every* s simply because the configuration appears so often (and correctly) in those genitive constructions. One can understand that kind of confusion, but it's still most unfortunate – and it comes about because the concept of the apostrophe as a device of omission has never been fully absorbed. A similarly comic but equally damaging 'knee-jerk reaction' characterises the second abuse.

2   **The apostrophe is not automatically used in words that include the successive letters '. . . nt . . .'**

It is therefore no less illiterate to write:

I **mean't** to write but forgot.   No, **Sergean't**, I have not been
                                        drinking.
The man **lean't** over the wall.   Are you going to the **pagean't**?

Again, it is not hard to see why these absurdities occur: it's because of such contractions as

can't   don't   won't   hadn't

– all of which use the apostrophe correctly. Writers who insert apostrophes in such instances resemble their 'greengrocer plurals' counterparts in their ignorance of the apostrophe's sole function: omission. Just like someone who instinctively writes 's regardless of context, they respond in a Pavlovian way to the mere sight of the . . . nt . . . formation, with laughable results.

Does it really matter whether we write these out correctly? Well, yes. Misuse of the apostrophe looks amateurish and often ridiculous, and nothing undermines a writer so much as seeming an idiot. But it can also confuse. It so happens, for example, that there are two nouns, **cant** and **wont**, that don't take the apostrophe:

1	**can't**	short for cannot. The apostrophe signals the omission of one **n** and the **o**.
1a	**cant**	hypocritical or spurious language; words used out of empty fashion/trendiness.
2	**won't**	short for will not. An admittedly odd contraction: the apostrophe signals the omission of the **o**.[1]
2a	**wont**	habit, custom.

Similarly, to prevent serious confusion one must distinguish between

3	**your**	belonging to you
3a	**you're**	a contraction of you are
4	**their**	belonging to them
4a	**they're**	a contraction of they are
4b	**there're**	a contraction of there are.[2]

So the apostrophe is a great deal more – and other – than an optional decoration. It is an aid to meaning and precision: remove it, and something valuable is lost, as this exercise should demonstrate.

Exercise 17

There follow three pairs of sentences. Each pair is identical save for the presence, absence or position of the apostrophe. Explain the consequent difference in meaning in each case. My 'answers' follow.

1a   The huge cliffs threatened.
1b   The huge cliff's threatened.

---

1   The change of the original . . . ill . . . to a single **o** was evidently considered too complicated to punctuate fully without tiring the reader and sacrificing clarity. Good thinking – as is **fo'csle** for **forecastle**. Strictly speaking, that contraction should be written **fo'c's'le**, but life is too short for such eye-straining fiddliness!

2   Perfectly correct but very rarely used – it looks (and indeed is) too cranky to be helpful. Stick to the full **there are**.

continued

2a He cares less about his children's welfare than his friend's.
2b He cares less about his children's welfare than his friends.

3a The village's well has been poisoned.
3b The villages' well has been poisoned.

Commentary on Exercise 17

Sentence 1a means that the cliffs threatened something unspecified – presumably a village, a group of people, or suchlike. Here **The cliffs** is the grammatical subject; the finite verb **threatened** is active in mood and in the past tense.

Sentence 1b means that something is threatening the huge cliff – erosion and/or the sea, perhaps. **The cliffs** remains the grammatical subject, but the finite verb has changed radically. The apostrophe signifies the omission of the **i**, making the verb **is threatened**: it is passive, not active, and in the present tense, not the past.

These are major changes in grammatical function and consequent meaning – all done by the briefest flick of the pen!

Sentence 2a means that he cares less about the welfare of his children than about the welfare of his friends. Put more simply, his friends matter to him more than his children do.

Sentence 2b means that his friends care more about the welfare of his children than he does. The difference here is perhaps less dramatic than in the first pair, but it remains a sizable one.

Sentence 3a means that the well which serves the (singular) village has been poisoned; 3b means that the well which serves *several* villages has been poisoned.

The difference in scale here is important. A poisoned well is obviously serious anyway, but number 3b could indicate a major disaster affecting villages and villagers for miles around.

The last of those three pairs illustrates the use of the apostrophe in plural possessives – the next problem area I want to consider.

The apostrophe in plural possessives

What's the difference in meaning here?

1 The boy's football shirt was filthy.
2 The boys' football shirt was filthy.

The first sentence means that a football shirt belonging to a particular boy was filthy. The second means that a football shirt belonging to several boys was filthy. Presumably they have to take turns in wearing it, while everyone else in the team wears a T-shirt or whatever!

After such a comically unlikely example, let's return for a moment to those Anglo-Saxon roots. You will recall that the genitive ending was originally -es; this applied in plurals as well. Thus:

the dogses bones   the Churcheses Bibles

In such cases the gradual erosion of the final syllable led to the dropping of the e and the s, creating the modern

the dogs' bones   the Churches' Bibles.

So plural possessives are, in the main, relaxingly easy: all that is required is an apostrophe *after* the s that signifies the plural number . However, beware of **irregular plurals**. We looked briefly at these in Chapter Five, and fortunately there aren't many of them; less fortunate is the fact that they tend to be in very frequent use.

Men's clothing   women's rights   children's games

These may be plural in concept but they are singular in grammar; they must therefore obey the singular possessive form.

Possessive adjectives and pronouns; its and it's

The apostrophe is never used in possessive adjectives or pronouns:

Adjectives: my; your; his/her/its; our; their; whose
Pronouns: mine; yours; his/hers/its;[3] ours; theirs; whose

---

3 Hardly ever used in this pronoun form, as it happens.

Only one of these causes trouble – **its** – but it does so in large measure. The problem arises because there is a form **it's**, and virtually everyone confuses the two at some time or another. Here are three separate recipes designed to dispel that confusion once for all.

A By now I will assume that you have nailed to your memory the fact that **all apostrophes denote omission!** If you keep that thought uppermost, the distinction ought to be clear:

> **its** = belonging to it; no omission has been performed.
> **it's** = it is; the second **i** has been omitted.

If that isn't clear, try the next.

B If in doubt as to whether to use **its** or **it's**, try mentally substituting **it is** in each case. If it sounds okay, then **it's** is correct; if you end up with gibberish, you must write **its**.

Examples:

1   The dog licked **it is** paw. *Obvious drivel: you need **its**:*
> The dog licked **its** paw.
2   I must say **it is** nice to see you. *No problem: write **it's**:*
> I must say **it's** nice to see you.

If that doesn't work, on to the final one.

C A four-stage 'theorem' – convoluted, maybe, but thorough:

1   **its** is the neuter equivalent of **his** and **her**.
2   I imagine you would never be tempted to write:
> **hi's or he'r**
3   So if you remember that the possessive its follows the same formation as **his/her**, you should now get that one right, and then. . . .
4   . . . remember to use **it's** in non-possessive contexts.

If none of those three recipes solves the problem, then I'm afraid there is nothing for it but to learn slowly by getting it wrong again and again until, somehow, it all sinks in!

The apostrophe with abbreviated verbs

In recent years a number of abbreviated verbs have become part of our language, and the apostrophe is a vital ingredient in their correct spelling.

1   She OK'd the merger.
2   He was KO'd in the fifth round.
3   They OD'd on barbiturates.

Unlike those illiterate plurals discussed earlier (**potato's, door's** e.g.), the apostrophe is entirely legitimate here. Indeed, it is **essential**: not to signal the dropping of the e invites the reader to 'mispronounce' the verb, with potentially confusing results. For if the e is signalled, explicitly or implicitly, one ends up with verbs which sound like

1a   She 'oaked' the merger.
2a   He was 'code' in the fifth round.
3a   They 'oded' on barbiturates.

I can't pretend that such instances would cause anyone a real problem for very long. But it's worth taking the trouble to present these abbreviated verbs in a clear and accurate way – partly because doing so confirms your mastery of the apostrophe and the reasons for its use.

I hope this section has demonstrated (better still, *confirmed*) that the apostrophe is a handy and badly neglected tool. Although it is true that your writing will be pretty proficient if the only errors you commit concern the apostrophe, using it properly will sharpen your work and add to your readers' precise understanding of it.

7.3 SYNONYMS: FACT OR FANTASY?

If my experience is representative, most children are introduced to the concept of the **synonym** in primary school, and by the time they assume secondary status they appear to be comfortable with the idea. That is both good and bad. It is good in that such young pupils seem thereby to have acquired an understanding of linguistic choice and of the enormous resources of the English language. It is bad in that such early training, however admirable, can induce a dangerously simplistic and rigid understanding of *meaning*.

For **synonym** is in fact a highly problematic concept. Here is the opening definition offered by the *Concise Oxford Dictionary* –

Word or phrase identical and coextensive in sense and usage with
another of the same language

– and that is the meaning most commonly assumed and applied. But it's
hardly ever as simple or clear-cut in practice, as this more detailed entry
in the *Shorter Oxford English Dictionary* demonstrates:

> **Strictly, a word having the same sense as another . . .** *but more*
> *usually either of any two or more words having the same general*
> *sense, but possessing each of them meanings which are not shared*
> *by the other or others, or having different shades of meaning*
> *appropriate to different contexts . . .*

(My emphasis)

As you might deduce from the italicised definitions, 'Full Monty'
synonyms are actually pretty rare. If you consult entry 32 in *Roget's
Thesaurus* you will find over a hundred related descriptors logged under
great, not one of which is an exact synonym of any other. Even if we take
five of the most obvious –

> **great**   **big**   **large**   **grand**   **supreme**

– they are by no means interchangeable, as can quickly be demonstrated
using this quintet of short sentences as our base.

1   She is a **great** writer.   2   I'll get my **big** brother onto you.
3   You are as **large** as life.   4   Their authority was **supreme**.
5   It was the most beautiful **grand** piano he had ever seen or heard.

In all five cases, none of the other four adjectives can be substituted
without a significant change in or even loss of meaning. You can test that
claim yourselves on Sentences 4 and 5 in a moment; first, let's look
together at the way Sentences 1–3 are affected.

In Sentence 1 the replacement of **great** by either **big** or **large** would
mean that the author in question is an ample[4] lady: we would learn

---

4   As you'd expect, **ample** also appears in *Roget's Thesaurus* entry 32. It is usually a phys-
    ical descriptor – **an ample room /garden/suitcase** – though it can be applied to certain
    abstractions – **ample scope/opportunity**. But it is not appropriate in *moral* or *aesthetic*
    contexts: **his principles were ample** sounds odd, as does **an ample dilemma**, while to
    remark that **Shakespeare's sonnets are ample** or refer to **an ample symphony** could
    only be justified if the intent were comic.

nothing about her as a writer from such substitutions. It might be argued that such descriptors referred to the size of her books, not of her person, but I'm not convinced. In addition, neither alternative is something I can imagine anybody saying.

'She is a **grand** writer' has two possible meanings, both entirely plausible. One is that she addresses huge topics and/or does so on an epic scale; the other is that her works are highly enjoyable, hinging on the (now distinctly old-fashioned) use of **grand** to denote 'very good'. Both make sense in a way that the previous two substitutions do not, but the real point is that neither means the same as 'She is a **great** writer'.

The substitution of **supreme** for **great** is the most interesting of all. Both resultant remarks are in the same area – that of artistic magnitude – but **supreme** is a more intense, even more congratulatory term. Indeed, it could even *supersede* **great**:

> Jane Austen is a **great** novelist, but George Eliot is **supreme**.

The opinion expressed there is of course open to argument, but the non-synonymous status of **great** and **supreme** is not.

Sentence 2 does not need anything like as much exploration – chiefly because in this case **big** has as much to do with age as size: the meaning implied is '*elder* brother' (hence, one presumes, bigger also). **Large** would connote *only* size, while **great brother**, **grand brother** and **supreme brother** are phrases that, again, I cannot imagine anyone ever using.

In Sentence 3 you could use 'as **great** as life' or 'as **big** as life', I suppose, but the force of the original phrase lies partly in its alliteration – the repetition of the l. Here **sound** is the key – as it is in the word **grandstand**, which is more effective than **large** stand or **big** stand could be even if all three do amount to the same thing.

Exercise 18

You might care to continue the above substitution exercise for Sentences 4 and 5 above. How many such replacements actually work anyway, and is there even one when meaning is unaltered? You'll find some suggested answers and commentary in Appendix II.

Their authority was **supreme**.
It was the most beautiful **grand** piano he had ever heard.

While it is, naturally, impossible to cover every aspect of this matter by focusing on just five words, I believe they exemplify not only the *partial* nature of the great majority of synonyms but also, and consequently, how much *care* is needed in choosing the right word. For as we've seen, it's not just meaning as such that counts: **euphony** is also an important consideration. There are many instances where **big** and **large** are indeed exact equivalents in terms of meaning, but their different sound makes each more appropriate in one context, less so in others. **Big** is a more aggressive, punchy word than **large**; so it makes sense to talk of someone being **big-headed** (conceited) but of someone else as **large-minded** (generous and imaginative). And you will find that such subtleties attend all other alternatives, no matter which section of the *Thesaurus* you consult. By all means make use of such a valuable aid, but don't ever stop thinking and listening when you do so.

Finally, there are also quite a few 'phantom synonyms' – that is, words that many people *think* mean more or less the same thing but which are completely separate, even opposites. On the assumption that you may have had enough of synonym-complexity for a little while, these are addressed below on pp. 152–5.

7.4 THE INDIRECT OBJECT

This has caused trouble to nearly everyone I've taught and deserves a section to itself. I would hope that by this stage you are clear about the **direct object**; just in case you're not, here are three further examples.

1 The boy passed **the ball**.
2 The inspector questioned **the suspect**.
3 He gave **five pounds**.

In each instance, the highlighted words are on the direct receiving end of the action defined by the verb. Now look at these more complex versions:

1a The boy passed **me** the ball.
2a The inspector gave **the suspect** a hard time.
3a He gave **Oxfam** five pounds.

In these examples the bold-type words form an **indirect object** that is dependent on the underlined direct object. In each case one could preface that indirect object with the word 'to', which confirms the suggestion of motion or transfer. Notice that in 2a, what was originally the direct object (**the suspect**) has become indirect: the direct object is now **a hard time**, given **to** the suspect.

If ever in doubt about which is the direct and which the indirect object, this simple test will help:

Which one can be left out so that the sentence still makes sense?

Check 1a, 2a and 3a in this way, and you'll quickly establish which is the secondary, indirect structure.

7.5 'WHICH' OR 'THAT'?

Which one will you choose?   That is the question

I only became fully aware of what a tricky issue this can be when one of my adult students, a Frenchman, asked for guidance on it. His EFL textbook covered the topic in some detail, but not enough to satisfy him – or when I perused it, me. I went on to compose an explanatory document for the whole class that drew more or less equally on that material and on *The Oxford English Grammar* (1996), edited by the late Sidney Greenbaum. An expanded version of that response now follows, since the problem seems to affect native and non-speakers alike.

Choosing whether to use **which** or **that** is in most cases a matter of style rather than accuracy, but that does not make it any less problematic. The key factor to my mind is the multiple function in English of **that**: it can be used in at least six ways. One of the six is as a *relative adjective*; **which** is also a *relative adjective*, and indeed is used *only* for that purpose.

It is likely that your head is beginning to throb somewhat already; however, there would seem to be a straightforward remedy. In view of the varied functions of **that** and its consequent frequency of use, it would be wise *always* to use **which** when requiring the *relative adjective*. But as you are doubtless aware by now, things are rarely as simple in English, and I fear this is another such instance. To solve the problem in full we need to approach it from four different angles.

Angle one

Some relative clauses give extra information. In these cases you must use **who** for people and **which** for things.

1 Yesterday I met John, **who** told me he was getting married.
2 She told me her address, **which** I wrote down in my diary.
3 The strike at the car factory, **which** lasted ten days, is now over.

That EFL textbook was adamant: *in these instances you cannot use* **that**. That injunction certainly holds good for 1 and 2, where the substitution of **that** for **which** sounds ugly and just plain wrong. But to write 3 as

3a The strike at the car factory, **that** lasted ten days, is now over.

seems much less ugly and indeed perfectly acceptable to my ears, rendering the proclaimed rule unsound, or at any rate not watertight.

Into this rapidly thickening plot we must now throw some further emulsifying agents – ingredients that *inter alia* show that there is no unanimity amongst the experts.

Angle two

For relative pronouns, the gender contrast is between **who/whom** and the non-personal **which**.

4 The friends **who** gave me advice
5 The teacher **whom** you just met
6 The book **which** I read recently

However, Greenbaum considers these next alternatives perfectly acceptable, as do I:

4a The friends **that** gave me advice
6a The book **that** I read recently

In siding with him rather than that EFL textbook, I am hardly making life easy for you: whom are you to trust? Well, as has just been implied, your chief ally will be your ear: go for the one which **sounds** 'right' or better. 4a and 6a sound fine to me, and I would be happy to use them as well. But if they seem at all dodgy to you, then pick **which** instead: you won't ever be wrong, just different.

Angle three

A situation can arise where both types of relative pronoun occur in the same sentence –

7   Tumours **which** grow slowly are less radio-sensitive than tumours **that** grow rapidly.

– and even modify the same noun:

8   There are two directories **that** I can direct you to **which** will help you.

The respective uses could be reversed with (in my view) no loss of meaning or euphony:

7a Tumours **that** grow slowly are less radio-sensitive than tumours **which** grow rapidly.
8a There are two directories **which** I can direct you to **that** will help you.

I can almost see the steam coming out of your ears, but try to relax and cheer up! The choice once again is *yours*; once again, too, the sensible option is to choose the one that pleases your **ear** more.

Angle four

There are some occasions when you may use either **which** or **that** but you will need to adjust punctuation and sentence-structure accordingly. Both the following say and mean exactly the same thing, but note the difference in lay-out:

9a Chimpanzees can grow as big as you and me, **which** is something that most people do not realise.
9b Chimpanzees can grow as big as you and me. **That** is something **which** most people do not realise.

Similarly:

10a He is at ease with the young, **which** is not true of all teachers.
10b He is at ease with the young: **that** is not true of all teachers.

Conclusion

Were this section on trial in a Scottish court, I'm fairly sure the jury would return that celebrated Caledonian verdict **not proven**. How best to use **which** and **that** seems to depend not only on which authority you consult but which country you happen to be in. And wherever you are, treat computer software with caution. Unlike dictionaries, computers have a tendency to bully you with their suddenly hectoring messages; try to ignore such bossiness, not least because

> **Computer software is only as reliable or 'right' as the human beings who designed and wrote it, and your own judgement and knowledge matter just as much if not more. Once you assume the computer can do your thinking for you, you are in big trouble.**

That especially applies in this instance, where the 'rules' are well nigh impossible to determine and where your own taste and sense of style are usually going to be what counts.

In sum: in dealing with **which** and **that** the wisest course is to take every instance as it comes, deciding each time on a one-off basis. In my opinion and experience, there are not all that many instances when you *must not* use **that**. However, as I remarked at the beginning, **that** is used multiply and often in English, so in most cases it is probably 'safest' to go for **which**. Finally, it may help you to consider the value of these relative adjectives as a *pair of alternatives*. If one or the other is occurring too often in your writing, you can vary it, preventing any annoyance on your readers' part at such frequency.

7.6 THE 'ULTRA-FORMAL REPLY'

I've included this brief section simply because a lot of my students have asked me about it over the years, and I don't know of any publication that deals specifically with it.

The ultra-formal reply comes into play when you're invited to a wedding, a coming-of-age party, a banquet (lucky old you!) or anything similarly grand and formal – the kind of occasion where a reply like 'Cheers for the invite – love to come' doesn't seem quite right! The convention instead is to answer in the *third person*:

> **Mr. and Mrs. Perkins thank Lord and Lady Culpepper for their kind invitation to the Graffingham Hunt Ball and are delighted to accept.**

If you have to decline the invitation, the pattern is

> **Raymond Lee thanks Mr and Mrs Newton for their kind invitation to their daughter Felicity's wedding, but must regretfully decline owing to a previous engagement.**

7.7 HANDLE WITH CARE!

This final – and extensive – section is offered partly in light-hearted vein, but it has a wholly serious purpose also. Although at times it may appear to have only a tenuous grammatical significance, in taking a look at words and phrases which should either be avoided or which are widely misunderstood and thus used incorrectly, it seeks to increase your awareness of certain traps that *anyone* can fall into if off guard. Effecting that should make you even more in charge of your writing than I hope you now are.

A living language can be compared to a river. It is never still and always changing: moreover, its survival depends on such fluidity. Thus every generation adds thousands of neologisms[5] to the language; during that period, too, many words and expressions will be imported from other languages; some rules and practices will also change. All that is just as it should be: as I remarked at the outset of this *Guide* –

> **Language – including and especially everyday usage – does not serve grammar: it is the other way round**

– and the health of any language depends on its being adaptable, supple and indeed *alive*.

Not all is vigour and productive invention, however. Just as every river has backwaters, many of which eventually dwindle into fens, puddles and mud, so every generation finds unique ways of rendering its language stagnant, opaque and disagreeable. This is perhaps most obviously exemplified in its clichés: notable culprits in our own time include:

> **at the end of the day; acid test; grass roots; green shoots; U-turn; skills;[6] in this day and age; healthy eating; personal organiser; road**

---

5   This term derives from two Greek words, **neo** meaning 'new' and **logos** meaning 'word'. A **neologism** is thus the creation of a new word or any new linguistic coinage.
6   What happened to 'knowledge' as the central requirement of learning and education?

rage; user-friendly; viable alternative; level playing-field; moving the goalposts; at this moment in time; parenting/to parent; cultural icon; the real world

and I'm sure you can think of many more. But no less injurious are those 'pools' of words that are used wrongly, inappropriately or ill-advisedly. Again, these are unique to each generation, and I trust it will prove valuable as well as amusing to look at some of the less impressive ways in which we write and speak now.

Words and structures to avoid

In *Write In Style* there is a whole chapter[7] devoted to such advice on how *not* to do it. The streamlined version offered here may duplicate a few of its colleague's examples or points, but it is newly written and designed to amplify rather than merely consolidate.

I start by taking a sour look at five individual words:

incredibly   literally   basically   definitely   pathetic

It is not the fact that nowadays they pepper both speech and writing that bothers me: such frequency may be tiresome, but it's hardly sufficient reason for devoting a whole subsection to them. What is important is that they are invariably used wrongly or with a complete loss of meaning.

My jaundiced views on **incredibly** extend to its 'brother adjective' **incredible** and to their equivalents **unbelievably** and **unbelievable**. All four hinge on the notion 'incapable of being believed'; the adjectives are instead used to signal anything from 'excellent' to 'mildly surprising', while the adverbs usually denote 'remarkably' or just 'very'. This is not only lazy – there are plenty of better alternatives – but reductive: if you regularly use **incredible** and **incredibly** in such a sloppy way, what have you got left to describe something that really *does* stretch belief to the utmost and beyond? The abuse is perhaps less objectionable in speech, where all of us can be imprecise or casual at times, but these words should never be *written* unless their true meaning is intended.

Literally means 'without mysticism, allegory or metaphor'; to put it another way, it exemplifies that modish acronym *WYSIWYG* – 'What You See Is What You Get'. In the four sentences which follow, 1 and 2 are therefore perfectly in order; 3 and 4 are not.

7   'Fight The Flab'; *Write In Style*, pp. 63–89.

1   Several casualties, unconscious but still alive, were **literally washed up** on the shore.
2   The window-cleaner had **literally lost his rag** and could not finish the job.
3   His career was **literally washed up** once he was found guilty of taking bribes.
4   At that point he **literally lost his rag** and threw the television set out of the window.

In 1 and 2 **literally** emphasises what really did happen – a passive journey to eventual survival and the loss of a vital piece of equipment. In 3 or 4 **washed up** and **his rag** are metaphors denoting 'finished' and 'temper' respectively, rendering the use of **literally** absurd.

As with **incredibly**, the misuse of **literally** stems from a failure to take any note of what the word means. The resultant assumption that it is a kind of all-purpose device adding decisive weight or colour can lead to statements that make 3 and 4 above seem almost sensible by comparison. Here are three such inanities as collected by *Private Eye* in its splendid 'Colemanballs' feature:

> **Many pilots shot down in the war were literally guinea pigs.**
> **Every time you pull on an England shirt you are literally under the microscope.**
> **You could literally hear the silence 50 miles away.**

To those can be added a similarly asinine instance which I heard while taking a short break from writing this very section:

> **Long-jump athletes are literally human kangaroos.**

Though equally undesirable, **basically** and **definitely** differ from **incredibly** and **literally** in that the problem is not so much illiteracy as uselessness. In most cases, **basically** is not employed – as it might legitimately be – as an alternative to **fundamentally** or **essentially** but merely as a form of trigger to get the speaker[8] started. In all these instances the word has no more authority than **um** or **er**:

1   **Basically**, it's all about commitment.
2   Astrology is **basically** a lot of nonsense.

8   Or, worse, the writer.

Pilots were literally guinea pigs.

3   **Basically**, what Shakespeare is saying in Hamlet is . . .
4   I'm interested, **basically**, in people.

In 1 and 2 **basically** is a form of verbal hiccup and does no work of any kind; in 3 it unwisely seems to suggest that an immense and complicated work can be summarised in a sentence or two; in 4 its use is so banal as to invoke laughter – unless the word is intended to denote 'on a primitive level', in which case the speaker might be someone best shunned!

   Definitely is similarly empty, but in a slightly different way. It is a curious word: although it is supposed to strengthen an assertion, the effect is often one of undermining. If you come out with something like

   Kennedy was definitely a tragic hero . . .
   Time is definitely relative . . .
   Genetically-modified food is definitely safe . . .

one somehow gets the impression that the matter is in doubt – that Kennedy was neither heroic nor tragic; that time is absolute; that genetically-modified food is decidedly dodgy. The emphatic tone causes a twinge of suspicion: the reader detects rhetoric, not evidence. Alternatively, it can carry an element of childish triumph – 'Wow! I've made up my mind about that, so there!' In any event, the word is hardly ever used beneficially; leave it alone.[9]

The problem with **pathetic** is that it has acquired two quite separate meanings. It derives from the Greek word for suffering, **pathos**, and signifies 'that which excites pity or sadness'. So in its original form **pathetic** describes anything that strikes one as forlorn, pitiable or distressingly moving. But it is now increasingly used to denote 'feeble', 'incompetent', 'contemptible' or just 'useless'. There's nothing I could do to outlaw such practice even if I wanted to; however, that street usage does mean that it is very hard to use **pathetic** in its classical sense without the high risk of being misunderstood. As a result, it is best to avoid it altogether: use instead a structure that makes use of the noun **pathos**.

As a postscript, I would like to reflect briefly on the word **love**. Unlike the other five, I would not suggest that you take steps to delete it from your written vocabulary: that would be ridiculous. But what a horribly *imprecise* word it is – which is both sad and amazing. I profoundly agree with Bernard Levin's assertion that the English language is the greatest work of art that mankind has (so far) produced; yet despite its vast riches we seem forced to use **love** in so many ways, so many contexts and in so many registers as to render it not so much seriously problematic as almost without meaning.

At one end of its ladder there are these words of Moses which even a determined atheist is bound to find impressive, if only because of their sheer scale and exclusivity:

Thou shalt love the Lord thy God with all thine heart, and with all thy soul, and with all thy might.[10]

At a slightly lower level **love** is used to define the greatest and most visceral human experiences – parental and filial love, sexual love, love of friends, the deep commitment to a walk of life/calling/career. Going down a considerable number of rungs, it also encompasses such

9   If you *must* use it, at least spell it right! It's **definitely.**
10 1611 Authorised Version, *Deuteronomy*, Chapter 6, verse 5.

enthusiasms as soccer or rugby – **I love Spurs / Wigan** – until one reaches the very bottom with expressions that are, frankly, ludicrous: **I love sausages / Diet Coke / Muesli yoghurt.** Moreover, such blanket usage has spread to the adjective **lovely** as well, so that (for example) it is a commonplace to be handed your credit card and bill at a supermarket check-out accompanied by the words, 'Thank you: that's lovely.' Credit cards, bills and indeed the business of household shopping can be a lot of things, including enjoyable; but they are not **lovely.**

It could well be argued that such eccentricity and daffiness is part of the charm of English; in any event, as with that street usage of **pathetic**, there's nothing one can do about the vagueness of **love**. However, I hope my frustration has at least amused you for a moment or so; if you share it, you might find the footnote below of interest and value.[11] Our focus now changes from individual words to similarly ill-advised larger structures.

Whatever you're writing, you can always assume that your reader is interested enough in what you're saying to give you a fair hearing, so there's no need to apologise for what you're about to write or to wind yourself up into it. Accordingly, avoid all these:

---

11 The Ancient Greeks seem to have understood very well – and very early – the kind of problems and resultant confusion that I've been talking about, for they divided **love** into four distinct categories. First there is *Agape*, which is spiritual love, including religious love. It often involves selflessness, even self-sacrifice: I suppose its highest, or anyway most dramatic, expression is to be found in Christ's

Greater love hath no man than this, but that he lay down his life for his friends.

The next is almost certainly the best known of the four – *eros*, which is physical love, especially (though not exclusively) *sexual* love. On the whole eros has had a very bad press (especially from those who regard *agape* as the highest form of love) and that may help to explain why it is probably the single most common and contagious source of human guilt.

The third category is **Storge**. This is family love, and it operates both between and across the generations. It can be limited to a close-knit circle that – in terms of deep and powerful feeling – excludes cousins and other branches of the family; in other instances, it may be a much broader, perhaps richer phenomenon. And finally, there is **Philia**, which is affection, friendship, 'liking'. You may have come across it used as a suffix, correctly as in 'Anglophile' (someone very fond of England) and <u>in</u>correctly in the structure with which we are all saturatedly familiar: **paedophile**. I say 'incorrectly' because the word should – indeed *does* – mean someone who likes children, in a thoroughly warming and admirable fashion. Any decent teacher needs to be a paedophile, in fact – though on reflection I'd rather you didn't quote me on that!!

It is interesting to note that . . .	Kills all interest at once.
It may perhaps be said that . . .	Well, why shouldn't it be?
It is worthy of note that . . .	Ugly, pompous and wasteful.
We can safely say that . . .	If so, why not just *say* it?
From certain points of view . . .	*Whose* points of view? Looks vague and timid.

I call such structures **leaden lead-ins**. They and others like them slow everything down to no purpose, creating a flabby and timorous impression; the attempt to cover oneself either wastes time or is annoyingly unspecific. And most important of all, they are structures that hardly anyone would write if left to their own devices: they have all been *taught* on the basis of 'this is the right way to go about things.' It isn't. Just get on with it: both you and your readers will have a much better time and lose nothing in the process.

Last of all in this subsection, a few observations about

trying to . . .

It would be unjust to call this modest structure **leaden**, but it is still almost always best avoided; like many uses of **basically** and **definitely**, it adds nothing of use and indeed indicates uncertainty. Look at these examples:

1   Einstein is trying to put over the point that . . .
2   Milton is trying to show that the Fall is not Eve's *purpose* . . .
3   By making the last word of *Troilus and Cressida* 'diseases', Shakespeare is trying to show us how reductive the world of that play has been.

In each case the use of **trying to** is inaccurate, and in an unfortunate way. It is not Einstein, Milton or Shakespeare who are making the effort; they managed – rather well! – to articulate the ideas involved. It is the *writer* who is struggling, and while that is entirely understandable, it is not a good idea to shift the blame in such a way even if it is done unwittingly. And although the colossal status of my three chosen figures may therefore exaggerate the kickback damage to the writer, any use of **trying to** runs that risk and is therefore best avoided. Keep it simple.

Some further common errors

Earlier in this chapter we took a detailed look at **synonyms** and at how the apparently straightforward notion of same meaning in reality turns out to be elusive, indeed questionable. Nevertheless, in most cases the term **synonym** remains a legitimate and useful one: the differences between the words in question are to do with **nuances** (shades of meaning) and these are subtle even though they are crucial. But there are some words commonly supposed to be synonyms that are no such thing.

Phantom synonyms

We noted a few of these in Chapter One – the incorrect conflation of **masterful/masterly**, **uninterested/disinterested** and **mitigate/militate**. Here are six more such pairs:

1	imply/infer	4	pacific/specific
2	callous/cruel	5	dependent/dependant
3	lazy/idle	6	principal/principle

It might be argued that 4, 5 and 6 hinge on mistakes in spelling rather than conceptual understanding, but they are nonetheless confusibles that lead to faulty meaning, so the end result is the same.

1 Imply and **infer** do go together, certainly, but as complementary components, not as synonyms:

> **Imply** means 'hint' or 'suggest' and is done by the *speaker* or *writer*.
> **Infer** means 'deduce' or 'gather' and is done by the *listener* or *reader*.

Many people misuse **infer**, including quite a number who think it a superior alternative to **imply** and therefore imagine that they're scoring a point by so using it. Just like the lordly misuse of **I** when **me** is required, this is mere snobbish drivel, indicating delusions of adequacy as well as of grandeur.

2 The confusion between **lazy** and **idle** may be less disagreeable but it is just as widespread. They are emphatically not synonyms: there is a crucial difference between

	lazy	*not wanting to do anything*
and		
	idle	*not having anything to do*

Here **lazy** implies criticism[12] whereas **idle** is a neutral observation. Both words have other meanings too: **lazy** can denote 'slow-moving' or even 'effortless', neither of which need be disapproving uses, while **idle** can also indicate something that is 'pointless', as in **idle speculation** or **idle gossip**. But they are not interchangeable, and it astonishes me how many school-teachers think otherwise. If a pupil is **idle**,[13] it's the teacher's fault! Should you require a proper synonym for **lazy**, use **indolent**: it may be rather an earnest alternative, but at least it's an accurate one.

3 Callous and **cruel** both indicate highly unpleasant qualities, but they are quite distinct. **Callous** means indifferent to others' suffering; **cruel** denotes active enjoyment of it. Another way of distinguishing them is that **callousness** is a *cold* quality whereas **cruelty** is a *hot* one. It is a moot point which is worse: it depends on the circumstances and your own sensibilities.

4 On the surface it seems weird that **pacific**, meaning 'peaceful', could ever be thought synonymous with **specific**, which means 'particular' or 'exact'. The cause of confusion here is lazy pronunciation. **Specific** is quite a demanding word to enunciate, and in the flurry of speech the **s** is often jettisoned; in those circumstances, anyone new to the word is likely to infer that it is merely a different meaning of **pacific** and proceed accordingly. The practice is thus perpetuated – literally by word of mouth – and although I confess to finding it a rather endearing error, it is still an embarrassing one.

5 The difference between **dependent** and **dependant** is technical:

dependent	*adjective*	Subordinate, subject, contingent
dependant	*noun*	One who depends on another for support

---

12 When a word does this or carries any other kind of negative implications, it is said to be used 'in the **pejorative** sense', from the Latin *peior*, meaning 'worse'.

13 Or **bone-idle**, as too many speakers seem to think is the mandatory phrase. It's time to put this dreadful cliché out of our misery: it is not only tedious but (as I'm attempting to demonstrate) ill-conceived and usually just *wrong*.

You are unlikely to need or come across **dependant** very often: the only time I see it regularly is on Tax Return forms and the like. But it is worth taking full note of its spelling, if only because the endings of all these other words formed from **depend** require an **e**:

dependency   independence   independent   independently

6 Finally, **principal** and **principle** may sound the same but have nothing in common otherwise. **Principal** can be used in two ways:

adjective	**chief, main, leading, first in importance**
noun	**boss, head, ruler; original sum invested**

Principle is used only as a noun, though it has several applications:

primary element; fundamental truth; law of nature; general law as guide to action; (*plural*) personal code of right conduct

It is all too easy to write one when you intend the other – I've done it myself. But the consequences of doing so can cause trouble rather than just a blush of embarrassment. If you write

The principal was flawed.

where you intended

The principle was flawed.

your readers will get the wrong message, probably then becoming confused, and it may take your argument some time to recover.

Synonyms, whether genuine or phoney, require constant care. But the same is true of certain individual words, our next category.

Single-word howlers

We encountered a couple of these in Exercise 1 – the misuse of **enormity** and **decimate**. Here are six more:

1	**Pressurise**	4	**Like** to denote *say*
2	**Notice** (as a verb)	5	**Proactive**
3	**Momentarily**	6	**Impact** (as a verb)

A pretty motley collection, you might think, and you'd have a point: their most immediate common factor is that they all do my blood pressure no favours whatever. But self-indulgence is not the chief reason for my assault: for a start, all six are remarkably ugly, and in addition they are constantly used either wrongly or without meaning.

1 **Pressurise** means 'to raise to high, even intense pressure', a process that attends the manufacture of fizzy drinks or the maintenance of normal atmospheric pressure in an aircraft cabin. It is erroneously thought to be also the single-word equivalent of 'to exert pressure on'. Illiterate enough if the object of the verb is inanimate (**lever, foot-pump**) it becomes gruesomely so when applied to human beings, who if **pressurised** would immediately die, and in explosively messy fashion. Besides, there was no need for this nasty linguistic hijack in the first place: **pressure** has always functioned as a verb in addition to being a noun, and that's the word to use.

2 The verb **notice** can only be used *transitively*:

He noticed **her smile.**
The detective noticed **that the footprints were uneven.**

In each instance the highlighted words are the *object* of **noticed**. The first is a simple adjective + noun, the second a noun clause, and their inclusion is essential. To use the verb without an object –

That stain doesn't **notice.**

is tackily wrong; in such cases, use **show** instead.

3 **Momentarily** is an ugly word anyway, but if you *must* use it, do so in the sense of 'lasting only a moment'. A different usage, denoting 'in a moment's time', has been creeping in of late, and it won't do. If you wish to express that latter sense, go for 'presently'[14] or 'shortly'.

4 I have no idea why the use of **like** to denote *say* –

So he, like, 'Where are you going?'
To which I, like, 'None of your business.'

14 Until quite recently, 'presently' meant 'immediately' rather than 'in a little while': any instance of the word in a Shakespeare play, for example, will carry that former meaning.

– came about, and in truth I don't *want* to know: I just want it to go away for ever. It is as hideous as it is unnecessary, instantly making normally intelligent, articulate people sound like imbeciles. As its isolation by the pair of commas might indicate, it is no more meaningful than **sort of** or **um**, and rather less defensible. It's bad enough to come across it in speech, but I've read several broadsheet interviews where its use is considered acceptable. It isn't.

5 Proactive seems to have begun life as an illegal immigrant from The United States. Instead of being summarily deported, it was enthusiastically granted asylum by the Civil Service, after which it soon took its place alongside **on message, up to speed** and **push the envelope** on the trendy jargon chart. They're all horrible, but **proactive** is the worst. I suppose it was coined as a contrast to *re-active* – i.e. making things happen rather than merely responding when they do; what, however, was wrong with such words as **initiative, instigate, imaginative or enterprising**? Be they noun, verb or adjective, those long-established alternatives can be worked into structures no wordier than

    I want you to be proactive on this one.

and a great deal easier on the ear, eye and brain. **Proactive** resembles the recent A2/AS A Level Specifications, London's new County Hall and the euro in reminding us that innovative change does not necessarily mean improvement, and to adapt a remark made by Mark Twain about Jane Austen (whom he detested) it would be a great pity if it were allowed to die a natural death.

6 Until about twenty years ago – in the UK at any rate – **impact** was a *noun* only.[15] If you wanted to use it as a 'doing word' (verb) you had to clothe it in such compounds as

    have an impact on   **strike with immediate impact**

However, latterly it has become not only a verb in its own right –

    This may impact on sales.

---

15 Except in the context of dentistry, where its use as a *transitive verb* denoted 'the wedging of a tooth between another tooth and the jaw,' and even there it appeared much more frequently in past-participle form (**impacted wisdom tooth**) than as a fully-fledged verb.

– but now a *transitive* verb to boot:

Poor preparation will impact your work.

I dislike these recent developments intensely. Both verb-usages sound harsh, even threatening, and while it might be argued that the concept of **impact** is precisely those things, I don't think that's true. As a noun impact denotes 'an observable effect', good or bad; its use as a verb signals only *damage*, perverting the notion of 'collision' on which the original hinged into something more akin to 'crushing'.

Though unrepentant in my antipathy to **impact** as a verb, I am clearly in a minority already, and it may well be standard usage before we know it. That reflection serves also to introduce the next category – words and practices that were considered unquestionably 'wrong' a generation ago but which, despite remaining controversial, have begun to acquire a degree of respectability if not outright acceptance.

Some bones of contention

1 Hopefully

As an ordinary adverb, **hopefully** is entirely unproblematic, indicating *how* a particular action was performed:

1   He opened the envelope hopefully.
2   They looked hopefully at the sky for signs of brightness.

The trouble starts when it is used like this:

3   Hopefully the bus will arrive soon.
4   'They will hopefully be gone soon,' she whispered.

Many people – not just purists and pedants – are enraged by such practice, finding it ugly, illiterate and confusing. In view of my above tirades about **incredibly, literally** and so forth, you may be mildly surprised to learn that I am not amongst their number .

Technically the prosecution is of course quite right. In strict grammatical terms, both 3 and 4 are a nonsense: a **bus** cannot experience hope or any other emotion, while in 4 the adverb is linked to the speaker, not the **they** whose departure she so obviously wishes. So far, so unanswerable. My (perhaps misplaced) tolerance of the usage exemplified by 3 and 4 centres on the fact that it does no damage either to clarity or euphony; moreover, in practical terms there is no perversion of sense. Yes, 3 seems to endow a bus with the capacity for hope, but nobody could really believe, could they, that the writer intended that meaning? The same principle applies to 4: it is obvious what the speaker means, and the worst you can say about either sentence is that each is slightly clumsy.

Used in such a way **hopefully** is the almost exact equivalent of the German *hoffentlich*, a most useful word that translates as 'it is to be hoped that'. In both German and English the single word is not only more economical but a lot less pompous: I'd far rather hear or read

> 3   **Hopefully the bus will arrive soon.**

than

> 3a **It is to be hoped that the bus will arrive soon.**

Anyone who at all times insists on 3a calls to mind those who think it bad form to begin a sentence with a conjunction or who religiously avoid ending one with a preposition. They can't see the wood for the trees, and it is no accident that their own prose is often devoid of both charm and matter.

2 Alright

Until the last decade or so, the use of **alright** to mean 'okay, adequate' enjoyed colloquial status only – i.e. you could use it informally or in dialogue, but in academic and other formal contexts it was outlawed. It appears that this 'rule' is weakening; if so, I'm rather glad. There was a time when **alright** irritated me on principle, but I now think it a very useful device. For those who (like me) insisted on **all right** in its place ignored one important thing: such insistence rendered **all right** potentially ambiguous – denoting either 'okay' or 'totally correct'. **Alright** may strike the pedants as a rather unlovely little word, but its discrete spelling valuably preserves a distinction in meaning, and as such it will go on getting my vote.

3 'Quote' as a noun

As I write these words, I've no desire to stop teaching, which I still enjoy immensely; however, if I had a fiver for every time I've instructed my students to remember that **quote** is the verb, **quotation** the noun, and to write accordingly, I could have retired to – maybe even *bought* – some idyllic Pacific island many years ago.

Well, I think we've lost this one. **Quote** is now used almost universally as both noun and verb, and although there are still some sticklers (chiefly markers of English Literature exam papers) who will insist on **quotation** for the former, usage has finally triumphed over formal accuracy. I regret that – mainly because **quotation** is a fine word in its own right, and distinctions are always worth preserving – but it's no longer something I feel very strongly about. The next one is a different matter.

4 Homophobia

I object to this trendy noun on two quite separate counts. First of all, it is used wrongly by virtually everyone. The Greek word **phobia** means 'a morbid aversion' or 'an irrational fear', as in **arachnophobia** (fear of spiders[16]) or **claustrophobia** (fear of confined spaces). It therefore follows that **homophobia** actually means 'the fear that one is homosexual oneself' – a common enough syndrome down the centuries, but something very different from 'hostility to homosexuals', which has become its contemporary meaning. In the same way, the adjective **homophobic** now translates as 'anti-gay' rather than indicating a secret fear about one's own sexuality.

As I observed at the beginning of this section, language is in a constant state of flux, and the changed meaning of **homophobia** would exercise me less were it not for that second consideration, which is that **homophobia** lends a spurious dignity to a phenomenon that is squalid and reductive. Instinctively aggressive hostility towards *any* group of people is not only abhorrent but the kind of thing that any healthy civilisation seeks to expunge. One of the ways in which you do that is to make such bigotry seem *contemptible* – and that is not achieved by using grand-sounding Greek-derived words. There are times when it is best to be blunt: if you mean 'anti-gay' or 'an eagerness to persecute homosexuals', then use precisely those terms, not **homophobic** or **homophobia**.

I freely recognise that most people who misuse these words do so in good faith. There is no sinister undercurrent or hidden agenda: they wish to find a way of describing something of which they disapprove in a way that causes a minimum of offence. Such well-meaning practice is nevertheless precarious, and can create more problems than it solves – which sets up this chapter's final section.

---

16 You might be amused by Barry Cryer's witty variant, **anoraknophobia**: 'the morbid fear of train-spotters.'

The evils of PC

More than any other age, it seems, ours is awash with acronyms and abbreviations, so it is somewhat bizarre that two of the more far-reaching phenomena of recent times should share the intials **PC** – the **Personal Computer** and **Political Correctness**. Despite the brief warning I offered a little while ago about the limitations of computer software, it is not the former but the latter that concerns me here.

The term **Political Correctness** was unknown less than a generation ago. It would appear to have first surfaced in the United States in the late 1970s; yet within a decade it had become a globally significant ideology. And as characterises so many ideologies, a movement that rapidly became repressive, even totalitarian, was originally inspired by the best of intentions. Initially PC gave a new and arguably noble dimension to the practice of **euphemism**.[17] It sought to ensure that significant minorities were given proper respect and a proper voice; it also looked to draw stern attention to prejudice and injustice. Those estimable goals gave rise to a new style, including much new vocabulary; here are two examples, taken from a brilliant guide to PC compiled by Henry Beard and Christopher Cerf:[18]

Face-ism   **The oppressive tendency of the dominant culture to present pictures of men from the neck up only, but to show the entire bodies of women.**

(p. 21)

Differently abled   **A non-offensive alternative to *disabled*.**

(p. 16)

The tough-minded idealism and sensitivity evident in both impress me, as do these vinegary definitions from the same source:

Unwaged labour   *Housework*

(p. 80)

White Power Elite   *The Establishment*

(p. 76)

17 'The substitution of a mild or vague or roundabout expression for a harsh or blunt or direct one.' If you are interested in this topic, it is explored in *Write In Style*, Part Two.
18 *The Official Politically Correct Dictionary and Handbook* by Henry Beard and Christopher Cerf (London: HarperCollins, 1994). Hereinafter referred to as 'Beard and Cerf'.

It is difficult to tell exactly when and why PC went wrong, but go wrong it did. Within a few years this kind of substitution was becoming not only commonplace but in some circles mandatory:

Motivationally challenged	*Lazy*
Charm-free	*Boring*
Alternatively ethical	*Dishonest*
Differently attractive	*Ugly*

and by 1990 one could come across an aeroplane crash described as a **controlled flight into terrain**, the phrase **no longer a factor** to denote 'dead' and – perhaps most unnerving of all – a serial killer referred to as **a person with difficult-to-meet needs.**[19]

Now, on one level all the examples cited so far are amongst all else very *funny*, and the possibility exists that all were coined with at least partly humorous intent. I would like to think that the case, especially as spoof PC translations have become almost a minor art form in *I'm Sorry I Haven't A Clue* and other such splendidly irreverent programmes. When you hear Dostoevsky's *The Idiot* 'softened' into *The Under-Achiever* or catch Paul Merton rechristening a famous Clint Eastwood movie as *The Good, The Bad and the Facially Challenged*, the temptation is to think the whole PC thing was from the start a wonderfully elaborate joke. However, I don't believe it. PC may have provided us with a rich seam of humour, but that is a by-product it neither intended nor would even understand.

This is not the place – regrettably, for the matter is as absorbing as fundamental – to mount a full-scale enquiry into the nature of humour. However, it *is* pertinent to observe that ideology and humour go together like a horse and marriage or are about as likely a combination as avocados and whelks. No ideology in history has been noted for its humour; furthermore, in almost every instance ideologies are by nature humour*less*, and the reasons for that are worth going into.

In his seminal 1953 essay *The Rebel*, Albert Camus noted that every form of fascism embodies contempt and an utter lack of tolerance for others, and that all totalitarian regimes or movements adopt an official language that is either academic or bureaucratic. Even more telling was his perception that all ideologies run counter to human psychology and, therefore, to ordinary or natural behaviour – which last concept includes speech and the use of language in general.

19 Beard and Cerf, pages 117, 124 and 89.

That trio of observations prompts the realisation – central to any consideration of PC – that all ideological programmes are *absolute* in nature. Even at their most well-intentioned and ostensibly enabling, they allow no room for manoeuvre. Their governing property is righteousness, and their ethos can be summed up in an expression all of us have heard rather a lot recently: 'You're either for us or against us.'

In the starkest possible contrast, the surpassing value of humour lies in its *relativism*. No matter how scabrous or dubious in taste, humour exemplifies an awareness of alternative takes on the world, that there is more than one way of seeing things as they really are, and that (in the words of Goethe) 'to be certain is to be ridiculous.' And as such it is a major moral force. I know of no finer definition of morality than this one coined a hundred and fifty years ago:

Morality, which is specifically human, is dependent on the regulation of feeling by intellect.[20]

That wonderful insight hinges on *balance*. Moreover, not only is such equilibrium impossible to achieve without the relativism that humour guarantees: it also could be said to define the very concept of 'a sense of humour'.

How does all that impinge on PC? Well, like any crusade, it was overtaken by excessive zeal whereby 'the regulation of feeling by intellect' went out of the window, replaced by literal-minded earnestness or, worse, the aggressive denial of freedom of opinion. To illustrate the first, here's a brief anecdote recounted a few years ago by a student of mine:

His mother, who was a social worker in Luton, was reprimanded for including in a Report she had written on inadequate housing conditions the sentence 'The future looks black.' Fuming with rage about this, she went into the canteen for a shot of caffeine, to be confronted by a notice on the counter which read, 'Please do not offend by asking for white or black coffee.'

---

20 By George Eliot, in her 1855 essay 'Dr Cumming'.

While of course recognising that what might be termed 'colour descriptors' are a sensitive issue nowadays,[21] I still find the episode depressing. However, its misplaced solemnity is no more than silly; these next examples strike me as a good deal more sinister.

Grammar is the arbitrary rules of literary procedure subservient to a sexist political agenda.

That was written by a member of the English Department at an American University. He further argues his case with this extract from his Department Policy document:

Being as grammar is nothing but an ethnocentric white patriarchal reconstruction of language, hopefully we can eradicate it in no uncertain terms from and in regard to the curriculum at present.[22]

On that dismal evidence I'd say he has managed to eradicate grammar already, from his own prose if nowhere else. But his derisory shortcomings in that respect cannot hide the doctrinaire certainty of his *tone*, which typifies the PC ideologue: once you're convinced you're right about something, you aren't going to rest until all others do what you say and think as you do. And if they *don't* agree with you, they are automatically racist, fascist, sexist, or all three.

There are two further things to examine about PC and its doxies. First – and it is not easy for an English teacher to say this – PC ascribes to mere words a power they do not have. It proposes that if you rename a problem, it goes away. Thus if you outlaw offensive racial descriptors, you abolish racism; if you call people **less able** or **under-achievers** instead of 'thick', you abolish stupidity; use **chemically inconvenienced** to replace 'drunk' or 'stoned out of one's mind' and you remove the dangers of alcohol and

---

21 I recently heard a radio programme in which a highly intelligent Caribbean novelist confessed to wincing whenever he heard such expressions as 'a black day' or 'a black mood'. This surprised me a good deal, since up to that point he had been very witty at the expense of those who see hidden prejudice in the most innocuous idioms. It was pointed out to him that the use of 'black' in such expressions has nothing to do with race, deriving instead from the medieval notion of **the humours**, where black was the colour associated with *melancholy*. As I shall be demonstrating shortly, that kind of historical awareness is conspicuously absent in PC's approach to language. So having said, the novelist was very far from being a PC apologist, and his discomfort was clearly genuine. As a result, I for one intend to be even more careful about such things in future, even if I am unrepentant in my response to that Luton anecdote.

22 Beard and Cerf, p. 26.

drugs; and so on. I hope I'm not alone in finding this indescribable nonsense, and it was nailed as such, albeit obliquely, by the American novelist Raymond Chandler long before PC reared its head. In this extract from *The Long Goodbye* (published as it happens in 1953, like Camus's essay) Phillip Marlowe is talking to a policeman friend:

> In one way cops are all the same. They all blame the wrong things. If a guy loses his pay-cheque at a crap-table, stop gambling. If he gets drunk, stop liquor. If he kills somebody in a car crash, stop making automobiles. If he gets pinched with a girl in a hotel room, stop sexual intercourse. If he falls downstairs, stop building houses.

At its most tawdry, PC's propensity to 'blame the wrong things' degenerates into lazy smugness, as P.J. O'Rourke has observed:

> Political correctness is about people trying to talk their way into heaven, cheap virtue. I could do something about racism, I could do something about the plight of the inner cities in America, I could donate time, I could donate money, but how much easier to say 'African American' instead of 'black' and feel enormously good about myself and feel I have accomplished something.[23]

Those remarks might prompt the thought that PC is contemptible rather than sinister, and that provided there are enough people like O'Rourke around to pour such dismissive scorn on it, there's not much to worry about. Maybe so; but to my mind PC represents a real and present danger, and in summarising my reasons to be fearful, I seek also to justify my use of **evils** in this section's title.

First, its stance is unremittingly earnest.[24] I've explored that aspect enough, no doubt, and all I would add is that if it were left to the PC

---

23 Interviewed in The *Guardian*, November 25, 1995.
24 The term **gravitas** is fortuitously germane here. I nearly included it on pp. 155–8 as a further instance of mistaken understanding, but decided against that on account of its decidedly esoteric status. As might be deduced, **gravitas** approximates to the English word *gravity* – but not with the signification that virtually all who use it seem to assume. It applies in the Galilean but not the Gradgrindian sense – by which I mean that it denotes an unquestionable and irresistible force and has nothing to do with drab solemnity. I stress that distinction because those who do misuse the word tend also to regard humour or any analogous lightness of touch as injurious to their credibility and weightiness. The only meaning of 'weight' informing **gravitas** is that of intellectual authority, prompting the pleasing thought that to misunderstand the word might also be to misconstrue what truly impresses – which is expertise, not self-preening seriousness.

cops, all jokes would be forbidden by law on the basis that even the most innocuous might offend someone, somewhere. Second, it de-historicises language, robbing it of all its life-giving fluidity and creative flux. Here, for example, is an English major (at Duke University) on the subject of John Milton:

> **I won't touch him, because I know what the guy was up to – he was sexist through and through.**[25]

It's not just that this 'drags history into propaganda and denies the humanity of the dead: their sins, their virtues, their efforts, their failures';[26] it's not even that my every instinct recoils from this meat-headed condemnation of one of the greatest intellects the Western world has known. It is that his frame of reference is both cretinous and stupefyingly arrogant – as if all that has been written, thought and said is answerable solely to the terms and criteria of a code of practice invented in the last ten or so years. I'd worry about that even if the code were a sentient and trenchant one; as it is, one wants to laugh, except that resultant sound would be as far from a satisfied chuckle as could be imagined.

Third – and perhaps most important of all – is PC's demented passion for the literal. The American poet Robert Frost once observed, 'Great is he who imposes the metaphor'; PC seeks to take it away, notwithstanding the fact that 90 per cent of our language is figurative. In that respect it resembles Orwell's Newspeak – and if you think that a touch melodramatic, I would make two observations. The first is that a quotation from *1984* outlining the ultimate aims of Newspeak forms the epigraph to Beard and Cerf's *Handbook* on which I have been drawing: they would appear to find the parallel no more fanciful than I do. The second is that as the great philosopher Confucius observed:

> **When words lose their meaning, people lose their freedom.**

No matter how accidentally amusing PC can be (something one could never say of Newspeak) both its purpose and its practice are inimical to all that is most precious about language. That's why I referred to its **evils,**

---

25 Beard and Cerf, p. 108.
26 The words are those of Robert Hughes, in *Culture of Complaint: The Fraying of America* (London: OUP, 1993), p. 120.

and it's also why an attack on it is entirely appropriate in a book about English grammar. For as I'd like to think I've proved by now, grammar enables language to grow and to flourish; it preserves clarity and nuance; it is – perhaps paradoxically – the single most reliable guarantor of that freedom Confucius cites. Even at its most benign, **Political Correctness** fudges meaning, obliterates nuance, sanitises and reduces; at its most pernicious, it not only looks to police language but imprison and even kill it. That is why it matters and why it should be fought by us all.

Coda

After all that, a little light relief might be in order! The primary purpose of this book has been to instruct you in as many facets of grammar and usage as can be encompassed in a slimmish volume. Underscoring that aim, however, has been a belief that grammar can be fun as well as fundamental; it would be nice to think there have been moments when you've seen that it can actually be *funny*. This last exercise looks to demonstrate all those points; though it first appeared in Part Two of *Write In Style*, I hope it also proves an appropriately entertaining way in which to close this survey.

Exercise 19

The piece of raw prose below can be correctly punctuated in two quite separate ways, resulting in two utterly different meanings. I shall label the first version 'Come-on', the second 'Kiss-Off'. Can you work them out? Your decisions begin almost immediately after 'Dear John,' which is the only structure common to both. The answers follow overleaf.

Dear John
I want a man who knows what love is all about you are generous kind thoughtful people who are not like you admit to being useless and inferior you have ruined me for other men I yearn for you I have no feeling whatever when we're apart I can be forever happy will you let me be yours Gloria

---

Answers

1 'Come-On'

Dear John,

I want a man who knows what love is all about. You are generous, kind, thoughtful. People who are not like you admit to being useless and inferior. You have ruined me for other men. I yearn for you. I have no feelings whatever when we're apart. I can be forever happy – will you let me be yours?

Gloria

2 'Kiss-Off'

Dear John,

I want a man who knows what love is. All about you are generous, kind, thoughtful people, who are not like you. Admit to being useless and inferior. You have ruined me. For other men, I yearn. For you, I have no feelings whatever. When we're apart, I can be forever happy. Will you let me be?

Yours,

Gloria

Appendix I
A Grammatical and technical glossary

Readers familiar with the revised edition of *Write in Style* might assume that this Glossary is merely a duplication of the one that appears there. It is not. That incarnation included a profusion of literary terms, many of which I've omitted here on the grounds that they have no direct bearing on grammar as such. In addition, I have added a comparably substantial number of linguistic and grammatical terms that do not appear in that companion volume. As before, I have drawn in part on the 'Glossary of Terms' listed in the *National Literacy Strategy Framework for Teaching* (1998), but in the main the annotation and examples are my own, as are a significant number of the entries themselves.

In the left hand column, italics indicates that the term in question is also glossed in the main text. In the right-hand column, a bold-highlighted term advertises further annotation elsewhere in the list.

abbreviation	A word which is shortened. This may be a word which has passed into common usage – *phone* for *telephone*, *fridge* for refrigerator, *bus* for *omnibus*. Other abbreviations may be **acronyms** – NATO/North Atlantic Treaty Organisation; *modem/means of delivering electronic mail*. And others have passed into speech or writing in universally-understood abbreviated form, such as three standard Latinisms – *e.g./for example* (exempli gratia), *i.e./that is* (id est) and *etc./and so on* (et cetera) – or *BSE/Bovine Spongiform Encephalopathy*. See also **contraction**.
accent	Features of pronunciation which vary according to the speaker's regional and social origin. All oral language is spoken with an accent (including **standard English**) and speakers may use different accents in different situations. **Accent** applies *only* to pronunciation and should not be confused with **dialect**.

acronym	A word made up from the initial letters of the phrase in question: SWOT/*Strengths, Weaknesses, Opportunities, Threats*; DRINKY/*Double Regular Income No Kids Yet*
adjective	A word or phrase added or linked to a noun to describe or modify it.
adverb	A word or phrase which modifies a verb, an adjective or another adverb.
affix	A **morpheme** which is not in itself a word but is attached to a word. See also **prefix; suffix.**
agreement	Linked words or phrases must agree formally with each other in terms of **number, gender** and **person.** For example: *The girls collected their belongings* (plural forms agreeing) or *Yesterday I began a new job* (agreement of words concerning time).
alliteration	A phrase where neighbouring or closely connected words begin with the same letter or sound: *several shining ceilings; one weird witch; big burgers banish the blues.*
ambiguity	A phrase or statement which has more than one interpretation. Often unintentional and/or the result of careless writing, as in this (authentic) headline – *Police Help Dog Bite Victim* – where the omitted hyphen between *dog* and *bite* has a ludicrous result.
anagram	A word or words made up from the letters of another word or words: *marriage / a grim era; carthorse/ orchestra; mother-in-law / woman Hitler.*
analogy	The perception of similarity between two things.
antonym	A word with a meaning opposite to another: *hot – cold; light – heavy; imply – infer.* A word may have more than one antonym: *cold – hot/warm; moral – immoral/ amoral; like – dislike/unlike.*
apostrophe	A punctuation mark indicating the omission of a letter or letters. Contrary to widespread belief (and teaching guidance) the so-called 'possessive apostrophe' is *also* an instance of omission – in this case the dropping of the **e** from the Anglo-Saxon-derived genitive: *the womanes handbag* becomes *the woman's handbag.*
appendix	A section added to a document offering secondary or illustrative information.
article	The most basic form of **adjective,** incarnated in two forms – the *definite article* ('the') and the *indefinite* ('a', 'an'). Separately and also, a (mini) essay, usually commissioned for a newspaper or journal.

Police Help Dog Bite Victim

assonance   The repetition of vowel sounds; sometimes this involves a **rhyme** or **internal rhyme** – *dream team*; *fine wine* – but assonance can occur in non-rhyming forms too: *crying time*; *cool dude*.

asterisk (*)   A punctuation mark used most often to organise text, highlighting a point explained or followed-up elsewhere. It may also be used to **euphemise** taboo or risqué words by replacing letters.

bathos   A dramatic (and usually deliberate) anticlimax, neatly enshrined in the phrase *from the sublime to the ridiculous*.

case   The relation in which a noun or pronoun stands to some other word or words in a sentence; in **inflections**, the change in the form of a noun which shows that relation. In English there are five cases: *nominative*, *vocative*, *accusative*, *genitive* and **dative**. All are fully glossed in the main text. See also **declension**.

clause   A distinct part of a sentence that includes a **finite verb**.

clause analysis   The breaking down of a **clause** into its component parts and their relation to each other. See also **parse**.

cliché   An over-used phrase or opinion. (From the French *clicher* meaning 'to wear away/wear down'.)

colloquial   Typifying speech/language used in familiar, informal contexts.

colon (:)   A punctuation mark used to introduce a list, a quotation or a second clause which expands, illustrates or demonstrates the first.

comma (,)   A punctuation mark orchestrating the relationship between parts of a sentence. Often abused, it is too weak a 'stop' to separate sentences and for all but the most assured punctuator is probably best confined to separating words or phrases.

comparative   A specific form taken by adjectives and adverbs – *neat<u>er</u>, <u>more</u> clever; <u>more</u> often, bet<u>ter</u>*. See also **superlative**.

complement   Meaning 'that which completes'; defines the **predicate** for all verbs of *being, becoming and appearing* which do not – cannot – take a direct object.

compound word A word made up of two other words – *football, binliner, seatbelt*. Also found in hyphenated forms – *drugs-related crime, a bitter-sweet experience*. See also **hyphen**.

conditional   A clause or sentence which expresses the idea that the occurrence of one thing depends upon another. This can be effected through the form of the verb itself – *<u>Should</u> it be wet, we shall hold the picnic in the Scout Hut* – or via **conjunctions**: *<u>If</u> you go, I shall be sorry.*

conjugation   The breaking down of the **inflections** of a **verb** into **voice, mood, tense, number** and **person**. See also **declension**.

conjunction   A word used to link **sentences** or **clauses** or to connect words within the same **phrase**; from the two Latin words *con* ('with') and *junction* ('a joining'). Their use is normally as straightforward as enabling, but sometimes the choice of conjunction can crucially affect – indeed determine – meaning:

                      He was in a good mood <u>until</u> Jane asked him to sponsor her.

                      He was in a good mood <u>so</u> Jane asked him to sponsor her.

                      He was in a good mood <u>because</u> Jane asked him to sponsor her.

contraction	Words which are shortened – *fax* for *facsimile*, *cello* for *violincello* – or through **elision** reduced from two words to one: *can't / cannot; could've[1] / could have; won't / will not*. See also **apostrophe**.
correlatives	Words or phrases used together, always in pairs, and so related that one component implies the other – *either . . . or; both . . . and*.
dash (–)	Used *singly* to indicate an (often significant) after-thought or *in pairs* as an alternative to brackets. See also **parenthesis**.
declension	The breaking down of a **noun** into its various **cases**. See also **conjugation**.
decode	To convert a spoken/written message into language readily understood. The process is as old as language itself, but at the time of writing mobile phone text-messaging is probably the most prevalent instance.
derivation	The tracing of the origin of a word or saying.
dialect	Regional variations of **grammar** and **vocabulary**. These change over time, naturally; some disappear, often with disturbing speed. Dialect should on no account be confused with **accent**, an apparently similar but in fact wholly distinct matter.
dialogue	A conversation – spoken or written – between two or more parties. See **duologue**.
digraph	Two letters representing one **phoneme**: ba*th*; br*ai*n; *psych*ology
diminutive	A term implying smallness. Most often employed as a term of endearment or fond familiarity – *my lovely baby-girl, Babs* (instead of *Barbara*) – but sometimes used as a tougher indicator of status: *starlet, lecturette, underling*.
distributives	Adjectives and pronouns that refer to each individual of a class – e.g. *each, every, other*.
double negative	(1) Illiterate use: two negative forms which effectively cancel each other out: *they don't go sit in no waiting rooms; I never took nothing.* (2) More subtly, a way of 'holding back' from a fully positive statement. *Not unimpressive* is less of a compliment than *impressive*, while *never untruthful* is considerably weaker than *always truthful*.

1   Not *could of* – possibly the naffest illiteracy of them all!

duologue	A conversation/exchange between *only* two parties. See **dialogue**.
elision	An act of compression whereby a letter or **syllable** is omitted or suppressed. All **contractions** involve **elision**, but the latter also often occurs in verse for reasons of scansion, as in these celebrated lines from *Macbeth*:

> *If it were done when 'tis done, then 'twere well*
> *It were done quickly. If th' asassination*
> *Could trammel up the consequence . . .*

ellipsis (. . .)	Signifies a place where something has been omitted, or there is a pause for (immediate) interruption.
embedding	Placing a clause within a sentence rather than appending it with a conjunction. For example: *Trevor lives in Luton. He is a dentist.* becomes *Trevor, a dentist, lives in Luton.*
epic	A poem or story relating the adventures of a heroic or legendary figure, often relating to national identity – e.g. Odysseus or Arthur – or even mankind itself (*Paradise Lost*). Usually as grand in size as in scale.
epigraph	A short quotation or motto placed at the commencement of a book, chapter, or essay. The most telling epigraphs signify something of central significance in the forthcoming material; one of the more dramatic and illuminating is *Vengeance is mine, and I will repay* which heads Tolstoy's *Anna Karenin*.
epitaph	An engraved inscription on a tombstone.
etymology	The study of the origin, history and development of words.
eulogy	Writing or speech designed as a paean of praise to a named person or thing. In the USA, it refers specifically to funeral oration.
euphemism	The substitution of a mild or vague or roundabout expression for a harsh or blunt or direct one.
euphony	The quality of sounding pleasant; hence the adjective **euphonious**, 'attractive to the ear'. A fundamental consideration in all writing and speaking, every bit as important as formalistic rules, sometimes more so.
exclamation	A sentence – or sometimes a single word – expressing emotion. Concluded by an exclamation mark.

exclamation
mark (!)

fact

figurative
language

finite verb

future in the
past

gender

Punctuation mark used to signify great emotion – joy, anger, surprise, humour, pain, so forth. Also often accompanies **interjections**.

Accepted, observable or demonstrable truth. Facts must be supported by evidence; without it they can only be granted the status of opinion.[2]

The use of metaphor or simile to create a particular impression, mood or effect. At least 90 per cent of all language – be it spoken or written – is figurative. The opposite of figurative is *literal* – and the fact that the latter accounts for less than one-tenth of our linguistic activity is one of several reasons why the incautious use of *literally* must be resisted!

A verb defined by a **subject** and also a **tense**: *They work well together; The army will attack soon.*

A tense formed when changing **direct speech** with a future tense verb into **reported speech**. Thus the direct *I will remember* that becomes in reported speech, *I said that I would remember that.*

In a specifically grammatical sense, the division of nouns into masculine or feminine forms. Universal in several languages, it is only occasional in English but still important when it arises. Gender in English manifests itself most frequently in personal **pronouns** and possessive **adjectives**; it also characterises *personal animate nouns*, some *inanimate nouns* and some *nonpersonal animate nouns*. All these and other relevant instances are covered in Chapter Five.

2   Those two sentences, a slight adaptation of the *NLSF*'s entry on **facts**, form a perfectly decent, dictionary-style definition. But to my mind the matter is much more slippery and difficult than they imply, and one needs to dig deeper, which I can best do by quoting the psychologist William James. These words were written ninety years ago, but they are just as relevant to our own time, and particularly to what any writer's life is about:

'Facts' themselves are not true. They simply are. Truth is the function of the beliefs that start and terminate among them.

That is very difficult: what it means, I think, is that the real significance of facts – of all data, if you like – is how they are interpreted, how they are used by an individual discerning human brain. That is how people arrive at the 'truths' which inform and direct their lives; it is also how they arrive at knowledge as opposed to mere information.

gerund	A verbal noun – i.e. a noun constructed from a verb. Gerunds invariably end in *-ing* and so need to be carefully distinguished from other such words that function as adjectives or part of a verb itself.
glossary	Often in **appendix** form, a list of technical terms (which can include abbreviations and acronyms) that the writer thinks may be unfamiliar to the intended audience and/or of confirmatory and referential help to those readers.
grammar	The conventions which govern the relationship between words in any and all languages. It is worth re-emphasing here a point made in my main text – that *grammar serves language: it is never the other way round.*
homograph	Words with the same spelling as another but different meaning: *the calf was slaughtered / my calf was aching*; *Are you going to welsh on that bet?/He is Welsh*. Amongst the more spectacular examples is *cleave*, which can mean either 'to cling to, adhere' or 'to split violently asunder': *His tongue cleaved to the roof of his mouth / You cleave my heart in twain.*
homonym	A word with the same spelling or pronunciation as another but different in meaning or origin. A **homonym** will be either a **homograph** or a **homophone** – sometimes *both*.
homophone	Words which sound the same but have different meanings or spellings – *read/reed, we're/weir, threw/through*. **Homophones** underscore most **puns**; they are also responsible for a sizable proportion of spelling mistakes committed by even the most literate!
hyphen (–)	The least powerful of all punctuation-points, but no less valuable for that. Its applications are various:

(a) To make a single word or expression: *well-known*; *index-linked*.

(b) To prevent ambiguity – *re-cover/recover*; *re-sign/ resign*; *correspondent co-respondent* – and no less useful in preventing a different aspect of reader-confusion: *co-operate* is visually much more congenial than *cooperate*, as is *re-entry* instead of *reentry*.

(c) To join a prefix to a proper name: *anti-Darwinian*; *post-Renaissance*.

(d) To clarify meaning: *all-consuming lust* as opposed to *all consuming lust*, where the first denotes intense passion while the second seems to signify some kind of sexual equivalent of McDonald's. Similarly, *twenty-odd guests* denotes something quite different from *twenty odd guests*.

(e) To divide words at the end of a line of printed text. Even the brightest writers/ editors/typesetters can make ridiculous reader-unfriendly mistakes here!

idiom	A non-literal phrase whose meaning is understood by the people who use it but cannot be inferred from knowledge of the individual words: *over the top*; *under the weather*; *beside oneself*; *out to lunch*.
imperative	A sentence which constitutes a command or a (strong) request for action. *Get out of here* is a direct order; *Please get me my tablets* is still a command even if the tone is much gentler. In the first person the effect is 'softer' still, but *Let's go to the pictures* still qualifies as an imperative.
infinitive	The root **mood** of a verb, usually but not always preceded by the **preposition** <u>to</u>. The infinitive comes in two forms, the **simple** and the **perfect**: consult the Index for their explanation in the main text.
inflection	An **affix** which alters a word for changing tense, number, part of speech, so forth: *walk, walk<u>s</u>, walk<u>ed</u>, walk<u>ing</u>, walk<u>er</u>, walk<u>ers</u>.*
interjection	An **exclamation** uttered by a listener which interrupts the speaker (sometimes oneself). Usually marked in the text by an **exclamation mark**.
intonation	The tone of voice selected by a speaker or reader to impart further information to the listener, adding a further dimension to the words themselves.
intransitive	Describes a verb that takes no **object**. See also **transitive**.
jargon	Language used by a particular profession or interest-group. May – sometimes deliberately – include vocabulary unknown to the non-initiate.
metalanguage	The language we use when talking/writing about language itself. This particular **glossary** is almost entirely **metalingual**.
metaphor	Any usage in which meaning is not literal, where the writer/speaker alludes to something as if it were

something else: *He is an ass; the ship ploughed through the waves; the rain was rodding down.* It has been illuminatingly defined as 'imaginative substitution' (Fowler). See also **figurative language**.

mnemonic
A memory aid. Particularly valuable when learning to spell – *a pie̲ce of pie; there is a̲ ra̲t in separate;* and *ne̲ver e̲at chips, e̲at s̲alad s̲andwiches a̲nd r̲emain y̲oung,* an imaginative formula to ensure the correct spelling of *necessary.*[3]

monologue
A text spoken by one speaker. Can refer to a formal dramatic piece or to a speaker who monopolises the conversation and/or never shuts up!

mood
The form of a verb which shows the mode or manner in which a statement is made. There are four: *infinitive, indicative, imperative* and *subjunctive.* All are fully glossed in the main text.

morpheme
The smallest unit of verbal meaning. A word may consist of one morpheme (*joy*), two morphemes (*joy'ous*) or three or more morphemes (*joy'ous'ly, penn'i'less'ness*).

morphology
The study of word structure.

noun
A word which names a thing or a feeling.

nuance
A shade of meaning. There is, for example, a subtle but decisive difference between *true* and *not untrue* or *authoritative* and *bossy.* The English language abounds in nuances, but while such richness is to be celebrated, it can also cause problems: see **synonyms**, both below and in the main text.

number
Singular or **plural** form. Straightforward enough, perhaps, but matters of number can occasionally ambush the unwary. Strictly speaking, *the army a̲re̲ retreating* is incorrect, since *army* is a singular noun, for all that it implies many – members. Similarly, one should write/say *Not one of us i̲s ready* rather than *Not one of us a̲re̲ ready.* See also **agreement**.

object (direct)
The recipient of an action in a sentence: *Fred caught the̲ ba̲ll; The bulldozer destroyed the̲ house̲.*

object (indirect)
A 'secondary' object identifying someone or something affected by the controlling verb. In *He played me a tune,*

---

3   If your problem is limited to remembering the number of times c and s appear, *one̲ cof-fee, two̲ sugars* might help.

it is the *tune* that is played, not the listener, but the latter is obviously involved. The indirect object can usually be prefaced (and thereby recognised) by 'to' or 'for' even when those words are not formally required. *He played (for) me a tune*; *She passed (to) him the salt.*

onomatopoeia   A word whose sound is the same as its meaning: *cuckoo*, *hiss*. Full onomatopoeias are rare, but English abounds in words that have considerable onomatopoeic properties, particularly those denoting anything violent – *crash, bang, wallop, crunch, crush, squash.* . . .

oxymoron   A condensed **paradox**, whereby two apparent opposites are deliberately juxtaposed so as to produce a third, arresting concept; among the most frequent instances is the term *bittersweet*.

palindrome   A word or phrase which is the same when read forwards or backwards: *mum; dad; rotor; pip; noon; Madam, I'm Adam.*

paradox   A seemingly absurd but on reflection well-grounded and illuminating statement: *It is a paradox that people's vices often derive from their virtues.*

paragraph   A section of a piece of writing, marking a change of focus/time/place/topic, or a change of speaker in a passage of **dialogue**.

parenthesis   A word or phrase inserted to explain or elaborate. May be placed in brackets or between commas or dashes.

parse   To resolve a sentence into its component parts and describe them grammatically. See also **clause analysis**.

participle   (1) Present participle. Invariably ends in *-ing*, but beware: such words do not always help form verbs. They can be independent adjectives (*a passing thought*) or **gerunds** (*bedding, kindling*). For a full discussion of these three forms, see Chapter Five above.

(2) Past participle. Usually ends in *-ed, -d, -t, -en, -n* and follows the words *has, have, had* or *was*. Like its (1) counterpart, the past participle can also be used as an independent adjective (*fallen* arches, *driven* snow, *past participle* itself!

passive voice   A sentence in which the subject is the person or thing acted upon by the verb rather than the one who performs the action.

pathos	That which excites pity or sadness. Hence **pathetic**, which is also used colloquially to indicate *feeble* or *useless*. As a result, that adjective is potentially confusing and needs to be deployed with great care.
pejorative	From the Latin peior meaning 'worse', this adjective draws attention to the use of a word in a derogatory or demeaning sense. *It was a most ambitious scheme* is neutral or even complimentary, but when Brutus describes Caesar as 'ambitious' he is using the term **pejoratively**, equivalent to 'power-hungry' or just 'greedy'.
person	A text may be written in

the **first person** (*I*, *we*)
the **second person** (*you*, singular or plural)
the **third person** (*he*, *she*, *it*, *they*)

personification	A form of metaphor in which language relating to human action, capability, motivation or emotion is ascribed to non-human things or abstract concepts: *Mondays always seem to be in a bad mood; love is blind; the branches bent down and touched the window-pane.*
phatic	Refers to speech where the *act of communication/ contact* is the key thing, much more significant than what is actually said. Everyday examples would include the words we use when introduced to someone, *How do you do?*,[4] going into a room and saying *Hello, it's me*, or (in the UK especially) remarks about the weather.
phrasal verb	A verb consisting of a root verb combined with another word or words. These can become both lengthy and complex in some instances: *I have been waiting for this since Thursday; He should not have taken that on so rashly.*
phoneme	The smallest unit of sound in a word. It can be represented by one, two, three or four letters: *go*; *show*; *though*.
phrase	Two or more words that act as one unit.
pluperfect	A past tense that in effect is 'twice removed': *He slept soundly after he had run the marathon.*

---

4   The longer I live, the barmier this structure seems. It is incomplete, mystifying gobbledegook, surely prompting the query 'How do I do *what?*' – and, maybe, the additional rejoinder, 'And mind your own business anyway.'

plural	The form of a verb, noun or pronoun which indicates that there are more than one.
portmanteau	A word made up from blending two others: *smoke + fog = smog*; *breakfast + lunch = brunch*; *sham + amateurism = shamateurism*.
predicate	The part of a sentence which is not the **subject**.
prefix	A **morpheme** which can be added to the beginning of a word to change its meaning: *in'finite*; *dis'appear*; *in'famous*; *ig'noble*; *mis'lead*.
preposition	A word describing the relationship between two nouns, pronouns, or a noun and a pronoun.
pronoun	A word used instead of a preceding noun or noun phrase to prevent or reduce repetition, thus improving stylistic flow and readability.
proverb	A saying which states a belief about the world: *once bitten, twice shy*; *look before you leap*; *pride comes before a fall*.
pun	A play on words; the use of words with similar sounds but different meaning to humorous effect. Often – mystifyingly – considered 'the lowest form of wit'. See also **homophone**.
punctuation	A way of marking written text to help (indeed *ensure*) readers' understanding.
question mark (?)	Punctuation mark used at the end of a sentence to denote a question.
quotation	The noun. But see immediately below . . .
quote	The verb. However, nowadays **quote** is invariably employed as a noun also, and while some sticklers consider that practice illiterate, usage seems to be triumphing. Even so, the distinction is worth remembering even if it is not always acted upon.
redundancy	A situation where a word does no work and is either merely decorative or (more likely) should be deleted. See also **tautology**.
rhetorical expression	An utterance in which the intended meaning is different from that which might be inferred by a listener unaware of certain linguistic conventions. For example, *Do you know his name?* is not an enquiry concerning the listener's stock of knowledge but a request by the speaker to be told that name. Many rhetorical expressions are questions disguising imperatives: *Would you like to be*

	quiet? means *Shut up*, just as *Where do you think you're going?* is in effect a command forbidding departure.
rhyme	Words which contain the same **rime** in their final syllable are said to rhyme: *frown/clown; fangs/ meringues; cheques/sex.*
rime	That part of a syllable which contains the vowel and final consonant or consonant cluster: *at* in *cat; ourn* in *mourn; ringue* in *meringue.* Some words consist only of rime: *eel, or, us.*
root word	A word to which prefixes and suffixes may be added to make other words. In *dependent, dependant, independently, dependable* and *depending* the **root word** is *depend.*
semi-colon (;)	A punctuation mark used to separate phrases or clauses in a sentence. Much stronger than the comma but weaker than the full stop, it is an invaluable 'stop'.
sentence	A unit of written language which makes complete sense on its own.
simile	An image comparing two things through the agency of *as* or *like*: *as* guilty *as* hell; *he drinks* like *a fish.*
singular	A form of a noun, verb or pronoun indicating that there is only one agent involved.
slang	Words and phrases used in an informal context, often linked with regions or used by groups of people as a kind of code.
speech	**Direct**: words actually spoken, as indicated by speech marks: *'Go away!' I yelled.*
	Indirect or **Reported**: The writer/speaker reports what has been said but does not quote it. No speech marks are necessary: *I yelled at him to go away.*
split infinitive	The supposedly illiterate practice of placing another word or words between the to and the verb in question: *to boldly go where no man has gone before* is a now-legendary instance. It should, admittedly, be avoided if possible, but there are times when the alternatives are less **euphonious** or fail to communicate the exact meaning intended, so it is unwise to be too purist about it.
standard English	The language of public communication, distinguished from other forms of English by its vocabulary and by the rules and conventions of grammar, punctuation and spelling. Contrasts with **dialect**, with archaic

	forms and global variations (e.g. Australian/ American English).[5]
subject	The agent in a sentence – i.e. whoever or whatever is 'in charge' of the verb.
subordinate	A grammatical structure that is dependent upon another one for its meaning fully to emerge. Most often used of a **clause**.
suffix	A **morpheme** added to the end of a word.
superlative	A specific form taken by adjectives and adverbs – *neatest*, *most* clever; *most* often, best. See also **comparative**.
syllable	Each beat in a word. Words with only one beat are *monosyllabic*; words with more than one beat are *polysyllabic*.
synonyms	Words which have the same, or very similar meaning.[6]
syntax	The grammatical relationships between words, phrases and clauses; also (more narrowly) to do with matters of word-order.
tautology	A word or group of words which uselessly repeats an idea already established, either through ignorance or carelessness: *new innovation*; *this is an annual event held every year*; *throughout the whole play*.
tense	The time-zone which a verb occupies, telling us *when* something is/was/will be happening.

5   Standard English has recently come under fire in a number of quarters as elitist, confining and uncreative; one does not have to denigrate any of the other manifestations of our language to find such a view pretty silly. As in so many things, the most productive attitude is 'both/and' rather than 'either/or'. Besides, like it or not, Standard English is more or less the required register for a host of situations, so any writer needs to be properly aware of it.

6   This is the NLTF's primary definition, and it is perfectly accurate. But as I observe in the main text, writers of English need to be careful about synonyms, not least because – such is the richness of our language – there are so many. In fact, the number of synonyms that have *exactly* the same meaning is small: most contain subtle differences, either in shades of meaning or when they can be most gainfully employed. To be properly aware of that means, amongst all else, that you will use a **thesaurus** productively and that you will never run the risk of assuming, for example, that all these 'synonyms' for *break* – *shatter, demolish, interrupt, crack, fracture* – are interchangeable, and that these sentences are anything other than comic idiocies:

  To make an omelette, first demolish four eggs,

  He interrupted his leg playing rugby.

  I shattered my journey at Sheffield.

theme	The subject of a piece of writing. It is a good idea to get used to citing **theme** rather than **subject**, since the latter has a quite separate grammatical meaning. The former will reduce any chances of confusion in either reader or writer.
thesaurus	A reference text which groups words by meaning. An indispensable aid to all writers, but one to be used with care and intelligence; see footnote 6.
tone	Modulation of voice (in writing too) to express emotion, opinion, sentiment, so forth. This is arguably the hardest property of language both to define and exactly recognise, but it is often decisively important. See also **intonation** and **voice**.
transitive	Describes a verb that takes an **object**; See also **intransitive**. The terms are not so much difficult in themselves as confusing in practice, since many verbs can be *either* transitive *or* intransitive according to how they are used. *I walked home* is intransitive whereas *They walked* the dog is transitive.
trigraph	Three letters representing one **phoneme**: h<u>igh</u>; ju<u>dge</u>.
usage	Refers to the way in which a word or a grammatical structure is commonly used; such practice may not be strictly correct but is so widespread as to be accepted.
verb	A word or a group of words that names an action or state of being.
vocabulary	A collection or list of words; the sum of words composing a language; the range of language of a particular person, class or profession. It is the third which is of chief interest here, mainly because virtually everyone has (1) an active vocabulary and (2) a passive one. The former is the number of words that you can use with certainty, comfort or confidence. The latter is the larger aggregate, for it adds words you may recognise when you hear or read them or whose meaning you can contextually infer, but which you would probably not (as yet) use yourself.
voice	(1) A grammatical term relating to verbs, which are placed in either the **active** or the **passive voice**. The latter is very useful in certain situations or contexts, but in nearly all good writing the active voice predominates.

(2) Less formal or precise, but still very important: the
sense a piece of writing gives of the author's
personality, tone, standpoint or point of view. All
good writing will communicate that authorial voice
in a fashion both clear and pleasing – which is one
reason why successful writing works equally well
when read aloud and *vice versa*. See also **tone**.

Appendix II
Answers to exercises

Note The answers to Exercises **1, 11, 12, 13, 15, 16** and **19** appear in the main text immediately after the Exercise itself. In addition, **exercise 17** is a learning-by-heart exercise and as such can have no 'answer'.

Exercise 2

A

1 Master**ful**, not masterly.
2 He found the green mamba, a snake, unexpectedly beautiful. *or* Despite its being a snake, he found the green mamba unexpectedly beautiful.
3 **Fewer**, not less.
4 Comma essential between **that** and **Philip**.
5 No apostrophe in cauliflowe**rs**; **either**, not neither.

B

	Main clause	Subordinate clause
6	Try again	if at first you don't succeed
7	I won't go out	until I've heard from you
8	I'll shut up	Since you are determined to go through with this
9	My spirits droop	Whenever I hear the word 'salad'
10	It might be better to give up	once you've failed three times
11	his dog leapt up in welcome	As he walked through the door.

C

12 Indicative
13 Indicative

14 Imperative
15 Subjunctive
16 Indicative
17 Imperative.

D

18 *Clothing* is a gerund; *running* is an adjective
19 Gerund
20 **Playing** is part of the verb *were playing*; *absorbing* is an adjective.

Exercise 3

1 Telephoned 2 Appalled 3 Was 4 Destroyed 5 Became
6 Tasted 7 Savaged 8 Has vanquished 9 Will be returning
10 Will disappoint.

Exercise 4

	Subject	Verb	Object
1	The bomb	destroyed	the house
2	The dog	bit	the postman
3	The postman	bit	the dog
4	The man	walked	–
5	The children	walked	the dog
6	The cheetah	ran	–
7	The lecturer	ran over	the main ideas
8	The bulldozer	ran over	the hedgehog

Exercise 5

A

1 Was shining; intransitive.   2 Burnt; transitive
3 Exploded; intransitive.   4 Bought; transitive
5 Hit; transitive.   6 Will be; intransitive

B

1 I am going to the shops.
2 The floods had been devastating.
3 They were appearing on 'Big Brother'.
4 He will have passed his driving test.
5 Julian will be seeing Susan every day.

C
1 Indicative   2 Imperative   3 Subjunctive   4 Indicative
5 Imperative   6 Imperative.

Exercise 6

A
1   The bird was swallowed by the snake.
2   The slates were blown off the roof by the gale.
3   The large audience was not satisfied by the band.

B
1   We would appreciate an early settlement of your account.
2   The treasurer embezzled the charity's funds.
3   Your Sunshine Tours representative has taken care of all travel arrangements.

C
1 Brought.   2 Committed (note the double t).   3 Gone.   4 hopped (note the double p).   5 Cut.

D
In pair 1a and 1b, there is a change in emphasis: 1a places the primary focus on the organisation, 1b on its corruption. The difference is subtle but definite, and determines the use of the passive or active voice, according to which focus is desired.

In pair 2a and 2b, the first is in the indicative mood, the second in the subjunctive. The speaker/writer of 2b sees the proposed action as much less likely than pertains in 2a.

Exercise 7

A
1 Common/concrete.   2 Proper.   3 Collective.   4 Abstract.
5 **Either** abstract (*state of mind, mood*) or concrete (*a weather front; sunk place, hollow*).   6 Collective.   7 Common/concrete.   8 Proper.
9 Common/concrete.   10   **Either** abstract (*seriousness*) or concrete (*weight, attractive force*).

B
   Four common/concrete nouns: **man**; **buses**; **taxis**; **hamburger**.
   (You could also have **traffic** and **eagles**.)

Three proper nouns: **Big Ben**; **Parliament Square**; **McDonald's**.
Two collective nouns: **gathering**; **fleet**.
Three abstract nouns: **indifference**; **fascination**; **interest**.

C
1 Catching the last train home.
2 The old man's delight in painting.
3 The name of that well-dressed woman.
4 That your writing style is improving **and** how hard you have worked.
5 That he has the most experience.
6 What they were looking for.

Exercise 8

1 Between you and **me**. . . .
2 She and **I** . . .
3 Pass me **those** socks. . . .
4 They think **she** is the only one **who** can do the job.
5 The rich don't care about **us** poor people.

Exercise 9

A
Relative: **which** (line 3); **whom** (l. 6); **who** (l. 8).
Demonstrative: **that** (line 1); **that** (l. 4); **those** (l. 7); **that** (l. 9).
Interrogative: **what** (line 1); **what** (l. 2); **who** (l. 5).

B
Sentence number 1 means that students who plan their work sensibly tend to be more successful than other students.

Sentence number 2 argues that *all* students plan their work sensibly, and that they are therefore more successful than all other people. Sentence number 2 is, of course, a preposterous claim!

C
1 All; most.
2 Fewer.
3 Many; much. The second one has to be **much** because the verb is singular; **many** would be correct if the verb were changed to **are**.
4 Is. **Not one** is the controlling subject, and is singular; **of us** is dependent upon **it**, so a plural verb is wrong.

D
1   **Whose**, not who's.
2   **You're**, not your.
3   **They** is inadequate: there is no way of knowing to which team it refers.
4   **Quite** is redundant.
5   **Smaller**, not smallest. In addition, of course, it is nonsense to talk of one **half** being bigger/smaller than another! The sentence needs to be entirely re-written.

Exercise 10

A
1 Panicked.   2 Swollen.   3 Beginning (note the <u>double</u> **n**)   4 Lay.
5 Lied.

B
      1   **Once** TV-AM broadcast daily. (The most economical way).
or 1   TV-AM broadcast daily **until it lost its franchise in October 1991**. (Much wordier, but more informative!)
      2   **On that occasion** we let them off with a caution.

C
1   Kisses; marches.
2   (The) Kennedys; verb changes to **were**.
3   Parties; guys.
4   Criteria; verb changes to **are**.

D
1 **Music** must be singular.   2 **Those** shears.   3 Spurs'.   4 Media's.
5 Children's.

E
1 Abnormal.   2 Inopportune.   3 Misspell.   4 Disarray.
5 **Disocc**iate.
   Disassociate does not exist, although the noun **disassociation** does. Apologies for the 'trap'!

F
1 Uneasiness.   2 Detestation.   3 Joyful / joyous.   4 Urgently.
5 Dependable.

Exercise 14

A
1 Simple.
2 Complex. **As . . . apprenticeship**: an adverb clause of **cause**.
3 Double.
4 Multiple.

B
1 She told her husband that he looked very ill.
2 He said that he had just been on the point of calling the police.
or 2a He said that he had merely been going to call the police.
3 The supervisor admitted that the girl had been there yesterday.[1]
4 The assistant promised the man that he would be with him in a moment.

C
Sentence number 1 is much the stronger: the speaker is about to embark on a very hazardous mission of some kind, and the remark indicates active worry, or indeed real fear.

Sentence number 2 is **conditional**: the implication is that the speaker is not going to do something so hazardous, and is assessing the chances of survival in a *theoretical* way.

D

1	Both:	a) May we watch television?	**(noncount)**
		b) How many televisions have you got?	**(count)**
2	Noncount.		
3	Noncount.		
4	Count.		
5	Count.		
6	Both:	a) Light travels at 186,000 mps	**(noncount)**
		b) Please turn the lights off.	**(count)**
7	Count		
8	Both:	a) The windows are made of glass.	**(noncount)**
		b) Have you washed up the glasses?	**(count)**

---

1 This is not entirely satisfactory. We need more context to establish whether the **she** is a girl, a woman or a female animal of some kind. In addition, **there** is very vague in this reported speech version, but no better alternative is available.

E
1   Faulty: suggests the speaker is a reptile.
2   Faulty: suggests the male speaker is a woman.
3   Both structures are correct.
4   Faulty. It *could* be correct if the speaker washes dishes for a living, but it's unlikely that this was intended!

F

1	**As does the sun**	*comparison*
2	**Unless you have immediate treatment**	*condition*
3	**So that could easily be found**	*purpose*
4	**When it rains**	*time*
5	**Even though at first sight it looks loathsome**	*concession*
6	**That they will not even answer urgent letters**	*result*
7	**Where the bee sucks**	*place*
8	**As you've been under a lot of strain**	*cause*
9	**In the way I showed you**	*manner*

Exercise 18

4   Their authority was **supreme**.
    It could be argued that all four replacements result in sentences that make sense and all therefore 'work'. However, I don't much like, nor can I imagine many people saying, either

Their authority was **big**   *or*   Their authority was **grand**

and so I'd reject them. In addition, neither conveys the same meaning as the original, an objection which applies equally to the other two substitutions, euphonious and feasible though those are:

Their authority was **great**   *and*   Their authority was **large**

5   It was the most beautiful **grand** piano he had ever seen or heard.
    Probably the easiest of the five examples I gave. **Grand** piano is, in effect, a technical term, and none of the substitutions sounds other than odd or indeed meaningless. **Great** and **supreme** cannot operate as descriptors of a piano, and while at a pinch one could speak of a **big** or **large** piano, it's hard to see why one would do so.

Appendix III
Further reading

I have remarked more than once in the main text that this Guide makes no claims to comprehensiveness. It would therefore be surprising – indeed perverse – if its concluding Bibliography were not analogously restricted. There are now a great many books which address Grammar and everything that stems from or impinges upon it, and I cannot pretend that I even know about (let alone have read) them all. What follows is a selective survey of works that both as a teacher and as the writer of this book I have found of particular value, and which can be recommended without reservation.

STANDARD DICTIONARIES

Oxford English Dictionary Still beyond compare, but beyond the pockets of most individuals! The *Concise* and, especially, the *Shorter* editions are excellent, and reasonably priced.
Oxford American Dictionary
Chambers' Dictionary
Webster's New Collegiate Dictionary
Oxford Dictionary of English Etymology ed. C.T. Onions
Collins Cobuild English Language Dictionary Cobuild denotes the 'Collins Birmingham University International Language Database and this dictionary is imaginatively and helpfully put together.
Roget's Thesaurus of Words and Phrases Various/multiple publishers.

SPECIALIST & 'ALTERNATIVE' DICTIONARIES

John Ayto *Twentieth Century Words* OUP
John Ayto *Register of New Words* Longman
Ambrose Bierce *The Enlarged Devil's Dictionary* Penguin
Bill Bryson[1] *Dictionary of Troublesome Words* Penguin
Jonathon Green *Dictionary of Slang* Cassells
Jonathon Green *The Cynic's Lexicon* Sphere
R. W. Holder *Dictionary of Euphemisms* Faber
John Seely *Oxford Guide to Writing and Speaking* OUP

MAJOR GUIDES

Fowler's Modern English Usage Revised by Sir Ernest Gowers
Oxford English Grammar ed. Sidney Greenbaum
The Right Word At The Right Time ed. John Ellison Kahn (*Reader's Digest*, 1985)
The Complete Plain Words Sir Ernest Gowers
Oxford Guide to the English Language
Cambridge Encyclopedia of Language ed. David Crystal

GRAMMAR, MECHANICS AND USAGE

Kingsley Amis *The King's English* HarperCollins
S. H. Burton *Mastering English Language* Macmillan
G. V. Carey *Mind The Stop* Penguin
David Crystal *Who Cares About English Usage?* Penguin
David Crystal *Rediscover Grammar* Longman
Philip Howard *The State of The Language* Penguin
Eric Partridge *Usage and Abusage* Penguin
Philip Davies Roberts *Plain English: A User's Guide* Penguin
O. M. Thomson *Essential Grammar* Oxford

---

1   The author is now (rightly) world-famous, chiefly for his superb travelogues. But the cited work is the first of his that I came across, and that is entirely appropriate, since his subsequent books – all of which are no less recommended – are rooted in his scholarly and passionate interest in the language of the English-speaking peoples of the world.

Index

Bold type signifies an entire section devoted to that topic. Readers are also referred to the Glossary that comprises Appendix I.